LIFE IN THE FISH BOWL

The harrowing true story of an undercover cop who took down
51 of the nation's most notorious Crips and his cultural awakening amidst a
poor, gang-infested neighborhood

TEGAN BROADWATER

Cover Art: Mark Moore, Xenn Creative
Copy Editing: Michael Precker, Jim Broadwater

Copyright © 2020 Tegan Broadwater
All rights reserved.
ISBN: 978-0-57866162-9

Culvert Publishing

DEDICATION

For the innocent children left parentless after these operations, the good law enforcement officers who battle each day to protect them, and for the invaluable, caring people who dedicate their lives to ending cycles of violence and recidivism.

For Holli - Thank you for making me see that my dreams were meager compared to this amazing reality with you.

TABLE OF CONTENTS

AUTHOR'S NOTE

The people and events in this story are real. Some names have been changed to preserve privacy, avoid liabilities or further prosecution, and protect the lives of those involved in Operation Fishbowl. Some of the language in this book is intentionally crass or grammatically erred, and the writing style may stir some literature-studious readers. However, this is the only way I could accurately depict the lives of those described in this insane but true story. Dig in.

Since my law enforcement incipiency, I worked toward creating an undercover assignment like this. I rarely, if ever, see any more old-school "deep cover" assignments like the ones I studied from the 70's and 80's. I spent much of my time researching the remarkable undercover work of guys from Mike Levine and Joseph Pistone to Jerry Speziale and William Queen. They rank among some of the world's best undercover operators. Some are fantastic authors as well. But they are the exceptions. When the stars align, and opportunities arise that allow great things to be accomplished, folks like this step up without hesitation. They conquer their foes with their alter-personas, who soon become one with who they really are. This is what I experienced. I don't consider myself on the same level of greatness as those I studied. I am very proud, however, of what the dedicated officers, prosecutors, and agents who helped me and I accomplished. My case (I deemed it "Operation Fishbowl") turned out to be one of the largest, most successful deep-cover gang and narcotic infiltration cases in a long while.

The decision to write this book was an easy one. As my experiences unfolded in this bizarre undercover gig, I began jotting random notes in the event I ever decided to formally memorialize them. It turned out to be a life-changing experience. The difficulty would be figuring out which stories to include in the book. Overall, Operation Fishbowl saw 51 gang members convicted, 41 of which were convicted federally. I chose to include specific stories referencing 27 of them to consolidate all the madness. There was just no way to fit it all in one book. I had also been approached and asked by hundreds of people asking how in the world a 6-foot-1, 225-pound blond-haired white dude like me could possibly infiltrate a tight-knit group of Crip gang members with a long history of leadership, structure, and organized violence. In this book, I describe the mentality, tactics, emotional control, and ignorance of inherent dangers I leveraged to get inside a segment of one of the country's most deadly criminal organizations, the Crip street gang. Furthermore, I'll explore what I learned about them as people. I'll even try to explain how and why some of these killers became my friends despite their criminal disposition.

Tookie Williams met Raymond Washington in 1969, and the two decided to unite their local gang members from the west and east sides of South Central Los Angeles to battle neighboring street gangs. The leaders prioritized expanding the gang's membership to increase its power. By 1978, there were 45 Crip-affiliated gangs, called sets, operating in Los Angeles. The gang became increasingly violent as it aggressively expanded its turf. By the early 1980s, the gang was heavily involved in the drug trade. Crip sets began distributing crack cocaine throughout Los Angeles. The huge profits resulting from crack sales encouraged many Crips to establish new markets in other cities and states. In turn, many young black men in different states adopted the Crips' name and lifestyle. As a result, Crip membership soared, making it one of the most significant street gang associations in the country: over 800 sets with 30,000 to 35,000 members and associate members, including more than 13,000 in Los Angeles. The states with the highest estimated number of Crip sets remain California, Missouri, Oklahoma, and Texas.

The 5-Deuce (52nd Street) Hoover Gangster Crips, a faction of the Hoover criminal gang in LA, is the only Hoover gang still identifying itself under the Crip name. They still sport the traditional Crip blue, along with the orange associated with the Hoover criminal street gang and have also spread to Texas in force via the drug trade.

Although Texas is the leading entry point for cocaine in the United States, one of the important goals I set for Operation Fishbowl was not necessarily to focus on confiscating giant loads of dope but to solidify strong cases from the inside of this violent sect of dealers. This would result in the most violent criminals being forced from the community and into long prison sentences.

I never set out to win the "War on Drugs." That would have been asking for trouble amidst failing laws and policies far beyond the scope of any one person. But I did set out to restore one gang-infested neighborhood in Fort Worth, Texas, plagued by violence, prostitution and dope. I set out to free those good people trapped in a hometown prison they could not escape. People who could not afford to up and move away, people who had lived there peacefully for decades, even young people who were trying to raise children amidst the worst possible environment to do so. From the fanciest gated community to the roughest, most ramshackle neighborhood, you can't eradicate dope, even though most narc cops might see a massive seizure as a good photo op. But I was convinced that the dope deal doesn't automatically have to allow violent gang members to cause true societal breakdowns by robbing, raping, assaulting, and murdering.

This is the story of my pursuit to save a neighborhood by way of one known as X-Man, the leader and organizer of the Crip organization I became a part of. And this is the story of the people I fortuitously came to know and appreciate. To this day, I still hold hope that the children left in this environment can somehow survive and succeed without responsible parents because they are in the game or prison. This operation left 104 children without a parent. While inside, I not only learned creative ways to accomplish police objectives, but I also learned how these human beings thought and why they did what they did. That was far more important to understand than any policing skill, and I hope that point is made clear in this book.

CHAPTER 1
"Off the Books"

Bug told me we could pick up the dope at Tre's house. This was almost too good to be true, because Tre had rules – and the main rule was that no one did business from his house. Keeping dope deals out of one's primary digs is a supplier's rule of thumb. Tre might not have been the biggest dealer or the smartest or – despite his occasional tendency to shoot people who crossed him – the deadliest. But he stayed with the rule. These dudes just didn't buy or sell narcotics or guns where they rested their heads at night. One police raid and they could lose all their personal swag – their cash, their rides, their big-screens. Not to mention their supply. Losing a supply was even worse, considering it came from someone higher up the chain, and it is not free. Although they refer to the dope business as their game, it isn't an actual game for these guys. It's a way of life and death. They play by rules set by OGs (Original Gangsters) dating back decades. Bottom line: lose a few kilos of coke worth $50,000 to a police raid and know that somebody will die for it.

And they have families to protect. Most of these entrepreneurs kept girlfriends and children on the side. Some of them even kept girlfriends on the side of the girlfriends. They still tried to make sure the real wife and kids were "safe" and out of the gang-styled, sociopathic, shoot-then-ask-questions-later game. It was, obviously, the classy thing to do.

Tre was a Crip, specifically a "Four Trey N-Hood" gangster (a Crip subset), who had a sensible demeanor but also possessed a side that made one wonder if he were genuinely crazy. He was formidable, too. At 6-foot-1 and 220 pounds, his dark skin and mass of jailhouse tatts accentuated his lean and muscular build. With his volatile temperament, he had racked up a lengthy prison sentence from which he'd just been recently paroled and had already retaken his position as a family heir to the cocaine distribution biz in his hood. He had also wasted no time asserting his gangster-style dominance upon his return as he launched rounds from an AK-47 into the home of a suspected rival. He was back in the game and was now as hard as ever.

This time, Tre made an exception to the house rule, which I took as a gesture of trust. This was a huge step for me. I would be OTB (my term for working off-the-books) on my own. No one at the Fort Worth Police Department knew where I was, what I was doing, or how I was doing it. I was going rogue, only with a disciplined focus. Tre was throwing me a bone, and I intended to fetch it.

I was a 36-year-old cop pretending to be 10 years younger. I had burrowed further inside the Crips than anyone had thought possible. For one thing, the Crips were notoriously suspicious of outsiders. For another, the Crips were black. And I'm white. Not just white, but pinkish pale with blonde hair. Yet I had worked my way in deep and wasn't leaving any breadcrumbs to find the path home, either. I was feeling my way through the ranks, leveraging my ever-important intuition and opening doors as I came to them.

At the moment, I was trying to raise Bug and keep a lid on my anger. I didn't like waiting around when there was business to be done. I kept blowing up his phone, growing more pissed with each number I punched. He was supposed to be the informant working for me, but he sure didn't act like it. I would have to put up with it, though. Even mediocre informants were hard to find, and Bug was good.

Finally, just after 10 p.m., he answered: "Yo."

"Bug, what the hell, dude?"

"I know, I know, I'm sorry. I got all caught up waiting on a friend for something."

A friend? Where did he think we were going, a picnic?

Bug said, "But I'm ready now, bro."

So was I.

Bug drove his car, and I drove mine, a dark Mercedes E-Series seized from an eccentric meth dealer a few years earlier. It screamed drug kingpin.

I played my part, too: baggy jeans, wraparound shades, and my baseball cap worn backward. On the stereo, I cranked one of my favs, Dirty Wormz. This put me into the mood I needed: mean, focused and aggressive. As always, I carried my Smith & Wesson .38 in the front of my loosely fitted pants.

We headed for the Fishbowl, a scooped-out hillside of curving streets on the east side of Fort Worth. The Fishbowl was once a solid working-class subdivision of small clapboard homes built after World War II. But over the years, it had deteriorated into a nest of gang killings and crack sales – the worst in town.

The playgrounds were empty by day and with the streetlights shot out, dark at night. Every month or so, a dead body turned up in a vacant lot or the trunk of an abandoned car. Fishbowl violence became such that most cops answered calls at least two-deep. Nobody wanted to go in there alone.

Fort Worth, needless to say, is not Los Angeles. It has no beach or palm trees. Its star power is growing but still pales in comparison, and the weather will surprise you no matter how hard you guess at it. It is a friendly town with subtle affluence and an understated business hub that grew the city under everyone else's nose. It's unfortunate reputation as a strictly Western town remains, but it is a lively, advanced, and modern city of just under a million people and growing. It does have, like every other large and thriving city, a hood with a booming drug trade. This, combined with the growth and understated persona, made Fort Worth prime territory for the West Coast Crips.

From their home base in South Central LA, the Crips expanded like fast-food franchises: test the market, develop a strategy to dominate the area, then bring in an effective branch manager.

An effective Crip leader had to be able to do at least a couple of things well: count and kill. To handle the Fishbowl and surrounding turf, the Crips had sent in a guy named X-Man.

X-Man was local. He and his understudies had gone west and trained in the business of dope and gun trafficking with a family connection in Compton, then come home to run the place.

Quiet, unassuming, and handsome, X-Man had the management smarts to grow and operate a sprawling enterprise staffed by street thugs. He had another advantage as well: he was a sociopath who would murder without hesitation. To date, he had notched at least five killings, three of which he carried out alone and two others via contract.

By this time, I had been chasing X-Man and watching his control over the Eastside Crip network grow for six years. I still didn't know as much about him as I wanted. But I did know this: X-Man was the head of the snake.

I knew the road to X-Man ran first to Tre's house. I gunned the Benz to a smooth 75 through light traffic. The sun had been down for a couple of hours, but the temp was still hanging in the high 90s. In the distant oncoming headlights, waves of heat ghosted off the pavement, dancing to the driving beat of my overworked stereo. As we approached, I turned down my radio, lowered my windows, and looked up to the heavens. "You helped me get here, so I assume you'll get me out!" I often threw out short, conversational tidbits to make sure my back was covered.

We made the Fishbowl in 15 minutes. My plan was a low-key transaction: score a bird (a kilo of cocaine), hang and shoot the breeze for a few minutes, then bolt.

My purpose tonight wasn't to bust Tre, who was the classic middleman: a few steps up from street dealer, but below top management. I was engaged in brand building, in selling my persona. I was Tee, a no-BS, cash-heavy guy from the rich side of town, with a long list of wealthy clients from uppity country clubs and west side inheritors. To dig deeper into the Crip hierarchy, I needed Tre as a reference.

The first sign that my plan might be screwed, though, came when I saw Bug get out of his car with Carlos in tow. This was the "friend" he had mentioned: Hispanic, short, quiet, and unassuming. Bug re-introduced him to me. We'd met several weeks prior.

We nodded toward each other in general respect. I was not pleased to see him again. Bug had filled me in on Carlos before. Working from Northern Mexico, Carlos had supplied half of South Texas with cocaine before he got too much attention from the feds and "retired." His business affiliation, Los Zetas, was responsible for thousands of drug-related kidnappings and murders, including police, politicians, and federal agents. They were famous for decapitating police officers and leaving their heads on the courthouse steps.

"This should be interesting," I quietly told Bug.

"Tee, he ain't gonna cause any problems."

"And you know that how?"

"Come on, he knows this business. He'll sniff out a set-up in a split second."

Well, okay, maybe. I had business to transact and needed to stay focused, so I said, "Fine," and led the way to Tre's place with my newly formed posse.

Tre's house sat next to a vacant corner lot full of trash. It was small and old, with a signature chain link fence in the front. The nearest working streetlight was half a block down, so it was dark. It was so dark I could hardly see my own feet. As we approached the humble abode, I calmly knocked on the burglar-barred front door.

Suddenly, the sound of rusted hinges and wood filled the air. The wooden door behind the bar cage swung open, and I found myself staring down the barrel of a shotgun. I recognized the guy holding it as Pimp, one of Tre's stooges I had seen while rolling around the Bowl the last few months.

I guess he had short-term memory problems. "Who the fuck are you?" he asked.

"Whoa, bro!" I held my left hand up as a gesture of peace while my right hand rested next to my Smith. "We've got business here," I told him. "Let me talk to Tre."

Pimp kept the charm coming. "You don't know who you messin' wit', white boy! You at the wrong house!"

I stayed cool, but he kept the shotgun fixed on me. He was trembling and sweating like a guy high on something and he didn't seem to hear a word I was saying. My tactical brain was engaged. If I couldn't get him to calm down, I would have to draw down on him. I mentally recited moving quickly, stepping to the side of his aim and hopping off the porch, forcing him to come out and get me. This would give him a difficult target to hit, and it would move his shotgun barrel away from my posse while I raised the .38 and drilled him a new eye socket - if he were stupid enough to pursue. The lights from inside the house shone into my face and caused me temporary night blindness, though. I was not in an advantageous position.

Even if I pulled it off perfectly, I would probably be hit if Pimp managed to squeeze off a shot. The spread of the shotgun pellets at this distance would make it almost impossible for him to miss me completely, no matter how bad his aim. The feeling I had while considering all this was, in a word, intense. While I stood there, I simply relied on Pimp not to shoot. All he had to do was pull that trigger before I decided to move, and I was toast. If I moved first, I would surely cause him to shoot, and someone would at least get hurt. I sided with patience and my calm demeanor since I had more people there to be concerned with than just myself.

So I was relieved when Tre came from the back of the house, racing to the doorway.

"Put it down, Pimp!" Tre ordered.

Pimp lowered the gun slowly and reluctantly. He didn't look happy to be doing it, either.

I said, "This ain't so great for business, Tre."

"We straight, kinfolk," Tre said. He unlocked the burglar bar door for us, saying, "Come on in," as if we had dropped by for cookies after church.

I walked inside, followed by Bug and Carlos. Tre paused and eyeballed Carlos suspiciously and asked, "Who's the caboose?"

This got Pimp going again. "Yeah, you Latin King wannabe motherfucker? I'll waste you right now! Get out my hood, man, you lost."

Many things mattered to someone like Carlos: power, money, and women, to name a few. But nothing mattered more than respect, and he was getting none. Pimp had no clue who he was dealing with. He may have driven by a few houses and fired into windows as ordered by some low-end neighborhood gang leader, but Carlos killed entire families. He was ruthless and was a boss to many.

Before I could step in and explain a little bit of this to Pimp, Carlos pulled a pistol from his waistband and charged Tre's boy. He pinned Pimp against the living room wall, jammed the pistol into his mouth, and screamed something in Spanish.

Pimp dropped the shotgun on the floor. I rushed over and stood on the barrel so no one could pick it up while I kept my eyes bounding about the room to stave off tunnel vision.

Tre and I pleaded with Carlos, but Bug could speak Spanish, so we let him do most of the talking. "Carlos," Bug said, "this moron is worthless. Wasting him wouldn't be worth time in prison. Besides, this is Tee's deal!" The sound of four desperate male voices in two languages demanding cooperation and the guttural screams being thrust from deep in Pimp's soul commanded the room. I don't know how anyone understood anything. I was almost certain someone was about to die. I just had to make sure it wasn't going to be us.

After an eternal minute of consideration, Carlos pulled the gun out of Pimp's mouth – hard. He left him spitting teeth and bleeding all over Tre's floor and couch.

Now it was my turn to step up. "Get Carlos outta here!" I screamed at Bug. "Are you freakin' insane bringin' this here, man? This is supposed to be a place of business!"

"Come on, Carlos! Sorry, Tee," Bug said. Everyone was still hollering as Bug led Carlos out the door. Carlos would later tell me he left without protest because he realized he had disrespected me by stepping on my deal. I suppose even mass murderers have some manners.

Tre's boy stumbled into the kitchen and bled into the sink. Far gone by now was any chance to complete the deal. Tre was tending to Pimp and I was worried about getting my crew out of the hood before any reinforcements showed up. For all I knew, the scene had put Tre in the mood to kill me. But I played it as if it were just another night at the dope house.

"Tre, I'll hit you and talk biz another time," I said in the flattest tone I could manage.

I wondered if this had been a deal-breaker—if I had just lost a critical link in my case. It might mean months—even years—of work were destroyed, and the thought of that made me feel like throwing up.

But Tre smirked and nodded. "Hit my cell in the mornin', Tee."

Piece of cake, I thought to myself, facetiously. I pointed to the kitchen and asked, "You need an ambulance for that fool?"

"I-on't eed no ambuance, uck you!" Pimp yelled with his new speech impediment.

"Tomorrow, Tre," I said with a subtle wink, and walked out.

On the books, this might have looked like a cluster. But I drove away with happy thoughts and renewed confidence. This deal itself on this night may have been shot, but somehow none of us were. And my street cred just rocketed to a new height.

What I couldn't have known then was how deep I would get and who I would become. What I would ultimately learn as the outsider going inside this deadly set of criminals is that sometimes you have to play. Sometimes you have to shatter a dope-house window with a bowling ball. Sometimes you have to beat a gangbanger nearly to death with your bare hands. You will know true love. You will learn to appreciate the very people you pursue. There will be many nights when you don't know who you are. And in the end, you may have to wait for the one man you're after – the one you've tracked so many years for imprisoning a neighborhood of poor, innocent people - and whose demise has become your obsession – to make a single, stupid, fatal mistake.

And then it's on.

CHAPTER 2
"The Unlikely Narc"

I wasn't one of those kids who dreamed of becoming a cop. In fact, what I wanted to be was quite the farthest thing from being a cop. I wanted to be a rock star. I was a member of Kiss for four years straight on Halloween. I was grounded for wearing lick-and-stick tattoos to church. I made a homemade guitar for my 5th-grade art class project using rubber bands, cardboard, yardsticks, and wildly decorative colors. I was serious. Following a feeble attempt at guitar lessons, I began taking drum lessons that year. Ace Frehley, the famous guitarist for Kiss, lived just a few miles from us in Wilton, Connecticut. On our way to church every Sunday, we passed by his home, which was more like my house of worship. My mother would roll her eyes in disappointment as I pointed it out as if it were the first time, every time. I was stage-ready.

By the time I hit high school, my family had moved to Houston, Texas. There, I studied under several terrific piano, vocal, and drum teachers like famed drum clinician Bobby Rock (Nelson, Vinnie Vincent Invasion, Gary Hoey, Lita Ford). I played for bands with much older African American cats like the great Preston Hodge, playing soul and R&B hits as the only white kid in the clubs where we gigged. This was super cool, as it allowed me to learn first-hand about other music styles, but also taught me about my bandmates' culture and how they experienced life. It was amazing to drive into the most crime-ridden area of Houston and rehearse without a single concern. These were my friends. There was love, music and life experience with every visit. The only drag was that none of my underaged school friends could ever come to see me play. It had pretty much become a secret life of my own. I also played in a band with my best friend, Sparky, and a freshly graduated bassist, Steve. It kept me learning and growing as a musician and as a man.

In 1987 I was accepted into the renowned North Texas State University music school (now the University of North Texas). There I studied music composition, music theory, music history, piano, and, of course, drums. Studying there under jazz drummer extraordinaire Ed Soph was a fantastic experience. Ed had played with jazz greats such as Arnett Cobb, Stan Kenton, Clark Terry, Randy Brecker, and Dave Liebman before settling in as a primary educator there at one of the most prestigious music schools in the world. The regimen there was brutal. I practiced six hours a day. That, combined with a full class load and playing gigs in Dallas and Houston until three in the morning to pay rent, almost kicked my ass. I had followed my buddy and bandmate Sparky there. Sparky was a super-driven guy. He inspired me to focus and practice beyond what would be considered "normal." By his third year, he was the top-rated guitar player there, playing in the famous "One O'clock Lab Band." He was my best friend. He now plays guitar with Lynyrd Skynyrd, and we keep in touch as often as two busy dudes can. Only my youth and sheer determination to succeed saved me during my rigorous collegiate routine of practice rooms, recitals, gigs, classrooms, beer, and some intermittent sleep. But I would apply the experience later.

After a few years, I took a break from school and took a gig with a Vegas-style show band that played the Caesars Palace resort circuit in Atlantic City and the Poconos. I was determined to experience life on the road, even if it involved cheese. That's where I got my first taste of gang violence.

First, I should note that I used to be peace-loving, chance-giving, and the personification of naiveté. I was brought up comfortably with two married parents and friends who shared my passivity. My boss at this new gig, Vinnie Romano, was an experienced Vegas singer and talented comedian fond of gold neck chains wedged within chesty tufts and, on stage, pink tuxedos. You always knew when he was within 25 feet as the air would thicken with the scent of cheap cologne and humor-laden foul language. He also was an aspiring mobster. I discovered that during my first week at the job at a resort called the Pocono Palace. During a break one day early in the gig, I overheard him on the phone screaming at the top of his lungs. "I don't give a shit who you are, motherfucker!" he said. "You're nothing! You know who I am! If you ever show your face again, I'll kill you myself!"

Vinnie slammed the phone down and told me he was dropping me at my cabin. We carpooled around the resort since I didn't have my car there. I hadn't finished the famous Philly Cheesesteak I was eating, either, but I decided not to bring that up in light of the phone conversation.

I hurriedly scooped up the remains of my half-eaten sandwich, got into his car, and then we drove. The trek was short - only a couple miles and then up the last wooded hill of the vast Pennsylvania mountain toward my cabin. The colored mountain scenery there was phenomenal. Being from highly populated Texas cities, I was used to flat, tan, and widespread. Just as we were about to arrive, a black four-door Cadillac sped from behind. Amidst plumes of dust and rocks, it slid sideways and stopped in front of us, blocking our car. It was just like the movies but without the advantage of fiction. I was freaked out. Young and clueless, I looked at Vinnie as if waiting for instruction – or a bathroom. Everything suddenly began to move in slow motion.

"Run for your door!" Romano screamed. My amateur ass just froze. I stared wide-eyed, and my jaw dropped in my best impression of a startled Grouper. Red-faced and in a panic, he popped the center console in his car, pulled out his Glock, and racked a round into the chamber. In front of us, big, husky, stereotypical Italian guys bailed from the Cadillac, taking cover. Although I felt like I was watching a movie unfolding before my eyes, my 21-year-old unarmed ass finally came to life and bolted the 40 yards to my cabin in 2.2 seconds without further prodding. I wanted to watch, but even then, I was smart enough to take cover away from the action. I waited and listened intently as they teased a reenactment of the final scene in Scarface. I hoped Pacino would handle it differently this time, though. Finally, I heard vehicles speeding off sans the sound of gunshots. I was relieved, but also absolutely shocked that this type of thing actually happened in real life. I was so naive.

Although no one was hurt, my curiosity was stirred. I had no idea the mob was real. But as I was soon to discover, it was real and thriving indeed.

The next day I walked two miles to a 7-Eleven and called Sparky back in Texas. I told him how strange it felt to find myself with a bunch of Italian guys who appeared to be real stereotypical mobsters and let on briefly about the incident. I explained how when I'd first arrived at the gig, I was briefed on whom I could speak to and whom to stay away from (mob family members) as if I were actually involved in some mobster role-play. I did tell him that I was truly concerned about the events of the previous day and how I realized the mob was not just "in the movies" or mere historical figures from the 40s, 50s, and 60s. I mean, I suppose I knew there were still actual mobsters, but I assumed they were limited to some faraway, crime-ridden Italian section of New York, and I certainly would never run into any! Alas, I had so much yet to learn.

Then came the kicker. Within 24 hours of my private call, alone, on a pay phone, and on private property – Romano was in my face. "Broadwater," he said, "don't ever mention the word 'mob' again. You don't know who you're dealing with here. If you know what's good for you, just shut the fuck up and do your job!"

"Whoa." I just sat there, totally dumbfounded. All I could think of was how he could have possibly known about my private conversation on a pay phone. I wouldn't even tell my family for fear of retaliation after this. Much of my clammed reaction was born of my insistence that my peaceful persona would persevere as it had through my youth. However, I wasn't entirely through with my Mobster 101 class. I would receive more verification soon enough. Still in a little denial and suffering from a case of 21-year-old dumbassity, my mind insisted I was an unknowing player in a lost scene from Goodfellas. That is until the Teflon Don showed up.

One night, just before our energetic, tux-laden musical extravaganza of a performance, Romano charged backstage toward me in a panic. I mentally rolled my eyes in anticipation of the drama. He cornered me with the most intense look since his near-shootout. As he spoke, I felt time slow to a crawl. The words he spit dumbfounded me. "Let me tell you exactly how you will greet Mr. Gotti. You will keep your eyes down and reach out your hand only if he offers you his. You will not engage in any kind of conversation whatsoever. Don't fuck this up, Broadwater!"

Man, I was growing tired of being passive. All he had to do was and reasonably explain his agenda and I'd get it. Instead, with his over-the-top aggressive approach, I was starting to internalize this stressed-out, frazzled, and abusive crap. It began to interrupt my sleep, and I was sure to break out my suppressed Rambo soon, annihilating all in my path. I breathed deeply and blew his crazy ass off. Wait. Did he just say Mr. Gotti? Like – THE Gotti?

Sure enough, Romano introduced John Gotti to the audience during our show and wished his ailing and hospitalized wife a speedy recovery. Nearly 3,000 supposedly normal people gave the most powerful mob boss in the country a standing ovation. And as was my fear, the man appeared backstage after the show. The familiar stench of cologne and hairspray filled the room as he walked up with his blazer open just enough to show off his gold and shook my hand. I did it just the way Romano had told me. And I decided: it was already way past time to leave this gig.

I put in my notice the next morning. My boss did not take that too well. He threatened to blacklist me and swore I'd never work in the music industry another day in my life. I'd given him six weeks' notice and knew I had to go regardless, so I grew some and stuck to my guns. After finding and working in a new drummer and preparing to play my last gig with the guys, I went to Romano's cabin to pick up my last paycheck. He was drunk, sweaty, and wearing only a bathrobe – totally his element. He decided to take this opportunity to scream for 10 minutes about how he never got enough respect. He was underpaid and under-appreciated. He worked himself into a spitting rage. The more he hollered, the more enraged he became with his imaginary insolence. Then, amidst his flailing rant, his robe fell open, exposing the full Romano. I'd finally had enough and, in a purposefully calm tone, asked, "Can we just get to what I was here to ask about in the first place? My paycheck?" Not a wise move in retrospect.

Romano exploded. He literally began jumping around the house frantically, slinging pans and plates about the room. Then he uttered something about his gun and disappeared into his bedroom. I intuitively headed for the door in my standard calm demeanor – only faster. Romano came up behind me with his semi-automatic .45 pistol as I opened the door. The ratcheting sound of metal on metal and the smell of a freshly oiled firearm filled my senses as he racked a round into the chamber. "I'm going to kill you!" he screamed.

I hesitated for a split second but didn't turn around. I continued to walk out. As Romano lowered his gun toward me, I kept walking at a reasonable pace, determined to prove I was cool and collected despite his insanity. I clenched my fists as I paced patiently away from the madness, fully anticipating a round would soon tear through my back. I don't think I took a breath for the full-mile walk. The further I walked, the quieter it became. And before long – albeit too long, there was silence. I had managed to skate this one...again. "So I guess that means I'm not getting my check tonight?" I muttered quietly in my best Arnold impression—screw passivity.

I returned to Texas transformed. For months, I had nightmares about strangling or stabbing Romano—murdering him in the most intimate of ways—producing short horror films from my subconscious that I had never imagined before. I started looking for people who could train me to fight. I needed to release some negative energy and gain confidence to carry it forward. Sadly, I had just lost some of my peaceful live-and-let-live attitude.

To solidify my disdain for gang violence, one night in 1995, my brother and I were surrounded by a bunch of morons looking for a fight as we left a nightclub in Fort Worth. Apparently, we had made the mistake of bumping one of them as we tried to depart through a crowded doorway. In the parking lot, ten angry guys tried to grab us before we managed to wrestle free and jump into my car. As I fumbled for my keys and started the car, they began to kick it and smash my windows, all but one – the windshield. That one was up to me.

I started the car and backed away fast. With my tires screeching through bellowed rubber smoke, all the attackers dispersed curbside except one bright dude. He stood between the open road and us. He raised his fists and yelled in moronic victory as if he'd just won a championship trophy by scaring us off of a ten-on-two fight. I stopped the car. The smell of burning rubber seeped in through the windowless doors as the smoke slowly cleared - faintly revealing the still-standing idiot in the road. He screamed into the heavens like the true drunk, rich white kid he was—a kid whose bravado was based solely on his ability to leverage his frat friends. He was so wasted he had no idea they'd bailed and left him to finish the now unwinnable battle they started. Now, he single-handedly barricaded my only route to freedom. I glanced over at my brother and slammed the car into drive just as he yelled, "Hit him!" We concurred: It's time to even the odds. I had floored it. As we approached the fool at about 30 mph, he jumped straight up. I guess he thought he could clear the car – but that white dude couldn't jump. His overconfident, super-frat powers failed him. I hit him at a good speed, and we witnessed his knees enter my car via the windshield. It shattered as he fell over the roof. Superman then dropped to the pavement, and my brother and I rolled home glass-free. That broken fool will remember our frat forever - Delta-Guy-Oucha.

And that was it. The final hit broke my innocence, produced a determined and untrusting mindset, and drew me toward releasing these wrongs from my psyche. I needed a better way than bar fights to channel my new attitude. I had one goal in mind. I dove into intensive street combative training and slowly developed some skills I could use. I wracked my brain for months until one crystal-clear answer occurred: the only thing I could ever imagine myself doing outside of the music business – the one thing that would lay the groundwork for responsibly righting wrongs, releasing negative energy, and helping others fight their good fight. In 1996, I cut my eight-inch locks and applied to the Fort Worth Police Department. I put my new focus to good use. After six solid months in an intensive and informative academy, I hit streets in blue but was as green as ever.

Like almost every rookie, I went straight to patrol. From the first day, I set my sights on doing two things as a cop: work undercover and kick in doors. That seemed like a place I would thrive and could do much good for whatever community I served. Every move I made as a rookie was calculated. I was a sponge, learning and building a resume that, one day, the Narcotics Unit wouldn't refuse.

After my first year, I was transferred, at my request, to the toughest beat in town, the southeast side of Fort Worth, which included the Fishbowl. Here, I learned to handle real criminals in mass. I used my newfound fighting skills against a burglar who attacked me with a hatchet he'd just stolen from someone's garage. I went with my shorthanded shift every Sunday to disperse anti-police mobs that regularly spilled out of a tiny club and blocked the streets. I disarmed a suicidal person wielding a knife with my baton, denying fellow officers an opportunity to shoot. I was routinely involved in exciting fistfights with suspects who were determined not to go to jail, which became a valuable experience in my learning and training processes. I was involved in vehicle pursuits and foot chases. I was shot at while breaking up a gang fight in a nightclub. Finally, during my foot pursuit of a fleeing kidnapper into the woods one midnight, amidst the loud, rotary winds of the police helicopter swirling as it shone its lights below, I navigated through the pitch dark, determined to snatch the punk up and paused. At that moment, I knew this was where I belonged. The new me was born. I was about to make the most of it, too.

CHAPTER 3
"Compton Moves West"

By 1999, after a prolonged pestering of my superiors to do so, I began writing search warrants for my patrol team. I worked in an area with a Weed and Seed grant – money from the federal government designated to provide a budget for qualifying agencies with high drug trafficking areas. It allowed the department at the patrol level to initiate drug cases and serve dynamic search warrants, which enabled us to assault a target by breaching the door and entering without knocking first. The area was deemed dense enough to justify our team hitting local dope operations while the Narcotics Unit focused on the city as a whole. My fantastic new job essentially was this: I would do surveillance to determine a target to hit. Then, I would make an undercover buy or instruct a confidential informant to make a buy from my target house, selling narcotics from inside. No later than the end of my shift, I would take the dope recovered from the buy to our crime lab, tag it as evidence, and request an analysis. Once the results came back and I confirmed the dope was good, I would write the search warrant, take it to a state judge, and get it signed. I would then conduct more surveillance to ensure the methods and operating times were correct. From that surveillance, I'd prepare an operational plan. I determined where, when, and who would hit this target in this plan. I'd assign everything, including the order in which my team would go through the freshly kicked door. I was learning fast and on the fly.

In Weed and Seed, we operated under the radar for the most part. We could take advantage of opportunities when gaining entry that other units, such as narcotics, could not because we had no standard operational procedures in place. We were all put through training to be certified to execute dynamic entry warrants, but that was about it. We instituted our own creative tactics born out of difficult situations, such as some of the projects that had steel door frames and doors, which proved insanely difficult to breach with a battering ram. So, we would leverage tactics like breaking and raking windows, then diving through them into our target one by one. We'd toss a fireman jacket, procured by my brother, who'd become a Fort Worth fireman, over the windowsill to keep glass out of our hands as we dove through. Or we would throw a bowling ball through a bathroom window as a distraction tactic to keep the bad guys from flushing evidence if we took too long to breach the front door. All that we did was done with good and productive intentions. Here, with only the most primitive equipment, I learned to be creative. And under fire, creativity and the ability to adapt and improvise are paramount.

Once a warrant was ready, I'd brief the team. The Weed and Seed team at that time worked the evening shift patrolling the streets, which ended around 10 p.m. Typically, the warrants were slated for later in the evening since the dope house activity was usually higher and the team was finishing its shift. They were typically served on Tuesdays and Thursdays due to the organized fashion of my weekly schedule. I would finish the buys on Monday and kick the door in by Tuesday night. I'd do more buys Wednesday and then kick doors on Thursday night. Friday would be a catchall day for follow-up paperwork. This became such a routine for me that after some time, I had three separate informants tell me that the word on the street was that you did not do business on Tuesdays or Thursdays in our hood. They all referred to these days as "Task Force Tuesdays and Thursdays." That was a hell of a compliment, but it forced me to focus on mixing up my timing – and my schedule. I couldn't afford to be predictable. Being predictable in this arena meant people would be killed. Our team was practiced and reasonably disciplined. Exciting and primitive as our operation seemed, this was serious business. We took our teams of 6-8 guys, geared up in helmets and raid vests (expired vests handed down by SWAT), and I drew up the plans from A to Z. We pre-planned and planned again in preparation for these dangerous events. A team had taken a shot at this grant several years earlier, and they experienced accidental weapon discharges and had two officers shot because of the extreme lack of discipline and organization. That's not to say we had not run into our share of dangerous situations, including barricaded subjects upon entry, unpredictable traps and reinforcements put in place by the bad guys, and tackling suspects diving for weapons. But predictability would not be an acceptable reason for getting my team shot at.

On February 23, 2002, I received a tip from an informant that an up-and-coming dope supplier and violent Crip gang member with California ties had been moving his dope through houses in my area. They called him X-Man, for "X-ing out" those who dared to cross him.

X-Man was recruiting local gangsters to go back to So-Cal with him for weeks at a time to learn how to run a criminal enterprise. He had familial connections there and was privy to the cutting-edge ways in which the dominant gangs were building drug empires with street-smart business tactics and ruthless violence against their rivals. I heard he was returning to Cali again and planned to take another two local bangers back with him for a couple of weeks. X-Man would soon become my nemesis. This would also mark the first time I would meet X-Man face-to-face, but certainly not the last.

I took advantage of my small window of opportunity to first meet this entrepreneur by surveilling the area as discreetly as possible. I narrowed down one particular block where I believed three of his houses were actively selling cocaine and possibly stowing weapons. Covertly trudging on hands and knees through overgrown alleyways, I navigated the old rundown hood that once was affluent. Now, all the homes were dilapidated, and there were fences around the front and back yards for extra security. The porches of my guilty parties often included additional patrols by pit bulls. Notably, the innocent, hard-working families left there to fend for themselves amidst these selfish fools could hardly afford reinforcements, let alone pets.

I scratched my warrant out, then called and met the judge at his garden home on the cozy west side of town. He was a very knowledgeable man with an appreciation for my ambition. Through the years, he mentored and taught me as much as anyone about the legal aspects of my operations. "The 'ole 'Four-Corners Rule' is always in effect," he would remind me. "If the pertinent facts are in your head but not within the four corners of this warrant paperwork, they are legally worthless. Specific articulation is an absolute necessity." I respected him greatly. I had to be particularly careful about including too much information regarding my informant and what he told me. Yet, I managed to include enough corroborated info to get the judge's signature of approval. This would soon all be used in court, which makes it public information. I could not afford to include details that might expose the identity of my sources, or they would be in certain danger. That night, I was good to go, and the judge signed off on my work.

I gathered and briefed my team at about 11:15. We crammed into the rundown raid van after spending 30 minutes trying to start the P.O.S. Each of my teammates entered the van in a specific way to bail out in a planned order. I stood at the front passenger side of the van as the guys filed in: Sean "Full-Blown" Blaydes, "Barney Rubble," "Agent Orange," "Darkwing," "PAB," "Ox," "YZ-80," "Clee" and "Stock-Boss." I accounted for each member before getting into the van myself. Now it was time. We drove toward X-Man's spot.

When we first left, it was always jovial. Guys would prod and prank each other—kicking one another squarely in the balls meant love was in the air. As we got closer to our target, however, all became quiet. Focus overwhelmed our wit. I prayed in my casually reverent plain-guy-to-plain-God manner. We were arriving, and this could be big.

As we pulled to the first targeted dope house, turned off the headlights and made our approach, our driver mistakenly stopped right in front of the house (as opposed to the plan, which was to stop at the house next door – out of direct sightlines). We were spotted right away. "Shit, a spotter," Stock Boss whispered at the top of his lungs. We immediately bailed out of the van into our tactical line and made our way to the door as quickly as possible while maintaining our quasi-grouping. As I stepped out, I caught the curb hidden in the darkness. My frigging ankle was torn, but there was no time for worrying. As my luck would have it, the dopers finished barricading the door just as we got to it.

"Police – Search Warrant!" Our man Ox slammed the battering ram into the barricaded door a good five or six times without so much as denting it. They had a "New York Stop" in place. A New York Stop is a 2-by-4 leaned up and wedged into another 2-by-4 that was nailed across the inside of the door, reaching to the floor, where another 2-by-4 is nailed into the floor, supporting the prop and providing a hellacious doorjamb! "Window!" I hollered, which was the command for the perimeter team to bowl a couple of frames through the rear bathroom windows. After 15 slams with Ox's 360 pounds, the door finally blew off the hinges. We stormed into the house. This was a dangerous situation. They had all the time they needed to arm themselves.

Inside, we found guys sprawled on the floor, face down, with crack cocaine thrown everywhere. One of them was X-Man. He was calm, cool, quiet, obviously experienced – and intelligent. This op was f-ed.

Sifting through the people and collecting evidence was the easy part. Actually putting a case on one of them that would stick at the District Attorney's Office would be next to impossible. Although the dope was there and X-Man had thousands of dollars in his pocket, no cases were filed. Our District Attorney's office at the time insisted we had solid evidence linking dope directly to a specific person since the residence did not belong to any of the detainees. Although there was dope within the care, custody, and control of practically everyone inside this house, in this case, the DA argued that one person inside that house could have thrown all the dope, which then landed within reach of every other "innocent" person in the room. In their eyes, proving which suspect was the dope-tosser was impossible. I knew who it was, and despite the cash in X-Man's pocket and my word-from-the-street info on him, they insisted we needed more proof to file a case. This would be another important learning tool for me. I had to find better ways to keep these guys from resuming business so soon after they were arrested.

Later, we hit the two other places that X-Man supplied on that street. In one, we recovered 15 handguns and assault rifles with Crip inscriptions on them, and arrested X-Man's girl, Reetha. Reetha was young and naïve at the time but would, years later, try to become the dope business "Queen-pin" herself. That stupid move would prove to be her demise.

At the third house, we recovered a decent amount of coke and arrested a guy named Benny Lemmons, a.k.a. "Lil' Kenny." Lemmons was a Crip who was moving and cooking dope for X-Man and others. His street name was initially curious, but you must realize that Benny starts with B. It's associated with the "Blood" street gang, and Benny was a hardcore Crip. Bloods and Crips are sworn enemies. As juvenile as it seems, these guys were really into this sort of thing, so Benny became Kenny, and, eventually, Lil' Kenny.

Lil' Kenny sold dope for the 4x3 Crips (a faction of the original East Side Crips of Los Angeles located on 43rd Street), but his main gig was robbing other bangers and dope dealers at gunpoint. He would take their money and dope, then resell the dope for cheap to unload it quickly. Everyone seemed to know this about him for some reason, yet despite this knowledge, they still accepted him. This method of making a living usually gets you nowhere fast, as you might imagine.

It was 2004, approximately six months before Operation Fishbowl's launch. Lil' Kenny had been stupidly robbing some of X-Man's runners. Moreover, he robbed X-Man's partner's mother, trying to get her to tell him where cash was stashed. Finally, Lil' Kenny lost his f-ing mind and robbed X-Man's family looking for the same thing. Understand that X-Man was not just your average small-time wannabe gangster. He was a killer, a trained California gangster – a leader. He had smarts and lots of money; most of all, he could and would command others to do any dirty work he needed.

Following the robbery of his family, X-Man was done with Lil' Kenny's antics. X-Man hired two young Crips, Daeqwon Robinson, and Rodney Jones, to murder Lemmons and his Crip-robbing cohort, who went by the street name TC. X-Man agreed to pay them $20,000 for their work. This amount was chump-change to X-Man, but it was a fortune to such ignorant, small-time, yet ambitious and determined criminals as these two.

In March 2005, Daeqwon and Rodney hid in Lil' Kenny's dope house and waited for him and TC to arrive. TC got there first and was immediately clubbed and shot dead with the assault rifle Daeqwon brought. They quickly dragged his body to the bathtub and stowed it there while they lay in wait for their real target to arrive. Lil' Kenny finally arrived some hours later. When he entered the house, the two gangsters confronted him. They cursed him and told him why they were there. The thoughts that crossed Kenny's mind then must have been priceless. He became irate and argued with them. That was not going to fly with these two. Daeqwon shot him, wounding him. Then Daeqwon shot him again, this time in the stomach – a truly painful injury. He was made to remember X-Man at every step of the process. In a vile finale, Daeqwon took the assault rifle and aimed it up Lil' Kenny's ass, all the while talking smack and hailing X-Man's powerful reach. Then he fired. Lil' Kenny was done in the most humiliating of ways. Street justice under X-Man was as brutal as it got.

Daeqwon and Rodney loaded the two bodies into their car, dumped them across town, and then burned down the house, hoping to obliterate the crime scene. Even so, both were soon arrested – and before ever being paid. The power X-Man wielded silenced the two hired killers. They stayed quiet about the real reason behind the murders because they knew first-hand what X-Man could do. They were willing to take this rap broke yet receive credit for the brutality they demonstrated to gain notoriety in the streets – and prison yards. In another injurious DA twist, these thugs were given extraordinarily light sentences. This job can be frustrating.

FORT WORTH — Prosecutors have officially closed the case on four men charged in the fatal shootings of two cousins inside an east Fort Worth house in March 2005.
Last week, three defendants arrested in the deaths of Torian Wiley, 27, and Benny Lemmons, 25, reached plea bargains with prosecutors and pleaded guilty to various crimes. [Daeqwon Robinson], 23, pleaded guilty to murder on May 19 in the death of Lemmons and was sentenced to seven years in prison. [Rodney Jones], 35, Robinson's brother who was acquitted of capital murder in November in the slayings, pleaded guilty to unlawful possession of a firearm on May 19 and was sentenced to six years in prison. Prosecutors charged Jones with the gun crime after he admitted, during his capital murder trial, to being a felon in possession of a firearm. Marcus Ray, 29, pleaded guilty on Friday to tampering with physical evidence for helping dispose of Wiley's and Lemmons' bodies and was sentenced to six years of deferred adjudication probation. He received his deal in exchange for his testimony against Jones and Robinson. A fourth defendant, Christopher Smith, 23, pleaded guilty to tampering with physical evidence and arson in December for helping dispose of the bodies and destroying evidence and was sentenced to six years of deferred adjudication probation. He received the deal in exchange for his testimony against Session.

Background:
According to investigators, the victims, Wiley and Lemmons, were selling drugs from a house that Wiley rented in the 1400 block of East Morphy Street. At about 2 a.m. on March 11, 2005, police said Jones hit Wiley on the head with a 2-by-4 and then shot him in the head because he believed that Wiley had been disrespecting Robinson, his brother.

Investigators have said that the two brothers — Jones and Robinson — then waited until Lemmons came to the house later that morning. Officials have said that, after Lemmons walked in, Robinson shot him with an AK-47.

Police have said that the brothers, with the help of Smith and Ray, cleaned up the scene, loaded the bodies into Lemmons' car, and drove it to the Como neighborhood, where they dumped Wiley's body in a vacant house in the 5100 block of Blackmore Avenue and dumped Lemmons' body in a vacant lot about 200 yards away.

After the two bodies were found, Jones and Robinson were arrested and charged with capital murder and murder, respectively. Smith and Ray were charged with tampering with physical evidence. Smith was also charged with arson.

In November, Jones was tried on the capital murder charge and acquitted after he claimed he wasn't there and had nothing to do with the slayings. Prosecutor David Hagerman said that the verdict limited his options on how to handle Robinson's murder case.
"When we plead a case like this, this is in no way indicative of how we feel about the victims or their families," Hagerman said. "It is just that when a jury passes judgment on the same evidence and finds a co-defendant 'not guilty,' it limits your options."

X-Man was not only responsible for this double murder but also for three other cold-case murders and an additional shooting that wounded a Blood gang member. To this point, though, no one had been able to pin the big fish in this organization that terrorized the east side neighborhoods. I was going to find a way to get these Crips off the street for good. I figured, if you can't beat 'em, join 'em…then beat 'em. How I would join 'em would prove to be no easy feat.

CHAPTER 4
"Becoming Tee"

By the time I transferred from Weed and Seed to the Narcotics Unit, I had quite a bit of good experience. Some of that experience was learning the selection process into this unit. It was my fourth attempt that finally landed the gig. They didn't see the value of taking a tall white dude – until now. When I interviewed this time, I had such a deep resume they had no choice. I had prepared, led, and executed nearly 500 dynamic search warrants. That's kicking-in-doors deluxe for a cat in patrol. I also had seven active informants that I could use at any time. And my limited undercover experience was vital. I'd proven I was able to buy dope in places where I had no business doing so – and I was self-taught. However, this new gig would allow me to learn from some great officers who had a more profound knowledge of the game, which I needed, particularly regarding working undercover. I just needed to be choosy whom I learned from – and the choices quickly became obvious. The opportunity to observe how others work undercover tells you a lot.

Many narcs will sit you down and tell you there is a certain way you work undercover in certain situations. They will try to tell you to "dirty" your car, or wear an earring, or grow a beard. They will tell you to act "schitzy" or talk with an accent. This is a crock. That's the beauty of working undercover to me. There is no right or wrong way, just the way that allows you to be the most at ease with yourself when you work. If you don't believe or have confidence in your alter-persona, how will you convince others who you are while under duress? This is one really valuable thing I learned while working in the Narcotics Unit.

To this very day, I have intrigued and perplexed officers approaching me and asking how in the world I managed to work undercover in an area where I stood out so much and where everyone entering is overly scrutinized. I tell them you have to truly believe you are someone else. I know that is stated, but it is apparently harder to do than it sounds. Look at how most cops work undercover, and you'll also see how not to do things. Many are so desperate to make a case that they're pushy and won't accept rejection. This is an immediate giveaway for bangers and dealers schooled in the streets. I not only accepted rejection easily but also proved myself to suspicious dealers. I was quick to go somewhere else with my money. I'd also talk them out of selling me much once they agreed to do business. I was always the one to slow things down and tell them to pump the brakes until I got to know them. That's how it's done in the street. Smart dealers won't typically meet someone once or twice and then start selling huge amounts, so why would I do that if I were posing as a dealer? You must be comfortable with your persona and not be afraid to fail as that person before you can even begin to penetrate such a wall of violence, drugs, sex, and anti-police sentiment.

The Douglas family had run the Fishbowl since the 1980s. A few of the family leaders were imprisoned on murder and drug trafficking charges in the early 1990s, but this didn't do anything to curb the operations there. They learned from their mistakes and pushed forward with a more calculated, violent, and now-educated approach. Over time, the Douglas family grew to huge numbers, and certain relatives holding different surnames came up into prominent roles – particularly in the Fishbowl.

By 2003, a city councilman received such an inordinate number of complaints from citizens in and near the Fishbowl that he called and met with our Chief of Police, Ralph Mendoza. Chief was already aware of the ever-growing violence and trafficking activity there. He knew something had to be done and instructed our Narcotics Unit supervisors to devise a plan to solve this longtime problem. The chief approved paying overtime to ensure adequate involvement. The plan was that for some months, the Narcotics and Gang units would head a detail that involved making traffic stops, executing search warrants, jumping out on dealers from unmarked vehicles, pulling over customers leaving the area, and collecting intelligence from wherever possible on the Fishbowl inner workings.

Arrests were made, and some intelligence was gathered, but it almost seemed the criminals were learning the specific law enforcement activities beforehand. This foiled any chance of this effort making true progress in combating the problems. None of the main players had been touched. I began to suspect this Fishbowl criminal network ran closer to home than I had ever imagined…and boy, would I soon learn just how right I was.

By the time 2005 rolled around, the Fishbowl had completely resumed its dominance on the Crime Analyst's map. The occasional search warrant was run down there, and several of the area patrol officers routinely cruised through or answered the huge volume of calls. But they didn't go hands-on with anyone unless they had an assist. This was the norm, but this was not acceptable.

A few law-abiding citizens lived in the Fishbowl as literal prisoners of the ironclad, gang-run neighborhood. They were the people who motivated me to keep working. No one deserves to live like that. Some even had children. Walking to school was not an option for those poor souls stuck in those illicit blocks. We didn't see bus stops, superhero backpacks, or science fair projects being lugged to the end of the block. Some were elderly, too. They just stayed inside and kept their mouths shut. The front porches were reserved for lookouts in this hood. If they complained, they knew there was a price to pay, and they were too old to protect themselves longer. Sure, there were churches and outreach organizations nearby, but they could only help on their own turf. No one was walking these blocks and preaching, counseling, mentoring, coaching or teaching. The largest percentage of the Fishbowl was corrupt, bloody, violent, sexually explicit, deplorable, and cursed. God bless the churches and charities that fight the good fight every day. Without them, things could have been even worse. But the only church that made its mark here was the Church of Hard Knocks.

It was March of 2005. I sat in my truck with a thoroughly sprained ankle from a pick-up basketball game mishap, yet I was still at work. I'd wedged my crutches between the seats like a partition. "Rabbit" hopped into my front passenger seat and reached over my crutches to set the quarter-kilo of cocaine on my center console. He had counted my $4400 cash earlier and had left again to retrieve the goods.

"This what you need, Tee. It just gets better from here, man."

"What's it tip at, bro?" I asked him as I put the coke on a digital scale I kept inside my console. It weighed out fairly, and once I smelled the coke through the baggie, I could tell we were good to go. I gave the bust signal.

"That's what I'm talkin' 'bout!" I said.

Within seconds, Task Force Officers in full raid gear were pointing guns at our heads and ordering us out of the truck. Rabbit whipped his head around to look at me and stared, eyes and mouth wide.

"Are they with you?" he asked with a look of total panic.

"No way! They don't look so happy, either!"

I opened my door as ordered by the officers and was yanked out of the truck by my supervisor at the time, Sgt. David Wilson. I was slammed to the ground and arrested. I had warned him earlier that my ankle was killing me. It was black and purple and swollen from sitting upright during this long, drawn-out deal, but this needed to look legit.

"Who brought the dope?"

My sergeant interrogated me in front of Rabbit as I sat handcuffed on the ground in front of the RaceTrac convenience store. I watched as patrons began to gather and gawk at me. I sat defeated and sweating from the heat creeping off the concrete – only in Texas would this kind of heat come in March.

"I don't know nothin' bout dope, sir," I replied. "I just met this dude a minute ago and I was gonna give him a ride."

I glanced over at Rabbit, about 20 feet away, but listened intently to the line of questioning the officers hit me with. I managed a wink as I pretended to know nothing in front of Rabbit. I was hoping he would stay relaxed enough to decide to give the officers good intel on his suppliers, thinking he could screw me and save himself. And that is precisely what happened.

Rabbit was taken to the other side of the parking lot, which was out of my view. I was yanked up and tossed into the back of a sweltering hot police car for hours as customers continued to gawk and gossip. My team of officers managed to locate Rabbit's supplier and set up a sting for him. It wasn't very fruitful, but it was worth the effort just to put that pressure on. Ultimately, Rabbit would take a 16-year rap in the state pen for this in addition to the many previous deals we had done together. I eventually worked my way up the ladder and would nail the two dealers over his head for even more.

I finished the undercover op on Rabbit and his suppliers. I had been buying cocaine from him for two months. But before Rabbit ever learned my true identity, or pled guilty, or got sent away to the pen, I would have an idea – the idea, in fact.

Bug had been my informant for nearly a year by this point. We'd worked a ton of deals together and we trusted one another. So, I met Bug at a bar in late March of 2005 to pitch this "brilliant" idea.

"Yo, If I could get inside the Fishbowl posing as a dealer, make some buys and build some relationships over an extended period, I could make a serious impact by taking out some of their key players from the inside. And, if all goes according to plan, I might be able to lay a devastating case on X-Man – you know he's the source of all the organized crime there."

I lifted my glass, swirling the golden-neat whiskey, ran my nose over it for a short whiff, and then took a careful sip. In the back of my mind, I hoped I could get inside the organization deep enough and that Sgt. Wilson would allow me the freedom to work on my own. I did have high hopes for a big, booming, successful takedown of the entire Fishbowl organization far in the back of my mind, but I preferred to think realistically and short-term at that point. Besides, I truly had no idea what taking down the entire organization entailed.

Anyway, once I finished my pitch to Bug, there was a pause. Bug was looking down toward his whiskey, deep in thought. I put my glass down and waited in silence for his response. After a moment, his shoulders began to bounce as I heard the distinct sound of choking.

"Dude, you good?" I exclaimed.

Bug looked up. He couldn't contain himself any longer. He busted out laughing – and I mean full belly-rolling, breath-stealing cackles filled the otherwise empty watering hole. It made me laugh, too. We cracked each other up for a long minute or two, or at least until my face hurt. Bug finally gathered himself and dried tears from his eyes with his sleeve.

"C'mon, bro. You know I got this. Crazy or not, I'm rollin' with or without you."

Bug looked down and shook his head, then peered at me through the corner of his red, watery eyes. "Tee, that – is a horrible idea. What time we roll?"

So, Bug agreed the idea was ludicrous, but importantly, he was in. One of the keys to gaining a bad guy's trust is having someone he trusts vouch for you. I thought that since Rabbit had just gone down but still had no idea who I really was, I could at least name-drop. I would use the same persona I used in Rabbit's case.

I was "Tee" from the west side near TCU (Texas Christian University – former home of the great LaDainian Tomlinson). I picked the west side so that when I came east to do business in the Fishbowl, I would not be viewed as a competitor but rather as an opportunity. However, new clients are not always welcome clients, especially if you aren't part of the Crip network. Fishbowl clientele ranged from the crowd of known street-level users and prostitutes to the dozens of small-time Crip hustlers, to the rare but significant big Crip players buying wholesale product in multi-kilo quantities. However, the higher the quantity, the heavier the scrutiny and, in turn, the prerequisite to be familiar ruled.

Conversely, the lower-level deals involved poor, struggling gangsters with little to lose. This meant significant danger for me at each stage. To mitigate some of that risk, I had some IDs with my alias already in place, reflecting my criminal probation for an aggravated assault. It would save me some trouble and perhaps lend me some street cred – though I rarely showed it to anyone. I planned to explain that I had a source on the west side that was busted by the feds, and I was looking for a new connection.

Although there were plenty of big, multi-kilo powder cocaine deals going down in the Fishbowl behind the scenes, most of the overt, street-level sales were crack. This presented a problem for me. First, I didn't want to go in appearing as a crack cocaine user, or the only people I would meet would be street dealers working for the bigger guys I wanted. In addition to that, the guys working the big money and larger quantities did not get high. They were businessmen. It would be like telling a starving person to take and deliver food for you. It's not a practical way to do business. That's why the organization thrived. It was surprisingly organized and run using just the right balance of business smarts, gang violence, and intimidation.

My getting in deep would have to involve some street dealers, though. I would ask them where I could buy some powder cocaine. Crack cocaine is powder cocaine cooked through an inexpensive and easy process that purifies and expands the cocaine into crack, sometimes doubling the original powder quantity. So, the object of asking these street-level crack dealers for powder cocaine was to get them to take me to their suppliers who had the powder before it was cooked into crack. For their help in introducing me to the suppliers, I'd buy some crack and promise to try to start moving a little in my hood so they could make some money off me. That way, everyone would end up selling to me, and I could start establishing some relationships and, more importantly, street cred.

This was my plan, and I hoped for the best. I sometimes caught myself overplanning and trying to be too creative for my own good, but it was my way. If I took this risk, I needed to know I had at least a chance to succeed and survive where no one else could. As I prepared to embark on my first swim through this infamous hood, I took a deep breath, smirked, and thought about how stupid this actually was. But it was indeed so stupid that it just might work. This was the last time I would ever reflect on this insane idea. I was all in. I was going to jump from the plane and never look back. Here I come, X-Man.

Operation Fishbowl was conceived.

CHAPTER 5
"Testing the Waters"

I'd already called two of my most trusted teammates to cover me this first go-round. I emphasized the importance of staying far away when I went in. They would listen to the transaction over cell phones and remain ready to rescue me if they heard the distress signal or anything else obviously imminent. It is a difficult position to be in when you are tasked with listening to a deal like this. They know I'll face delicate situations such as guns being pulled, volatile attitudes, and criminal conversation, but they have to trust that I'll give the signal if I need them. Otherwise, the operation could end before it starts. On the other hand, my safety depends on knowing that if they hear something restricting my ability to call for help, they'll swoop in for a rescue without hesitation. These types of operations require a lot of faith in your brothers.

I found myself in the all-too-familiar position of sitting in Bug's driveway, waiting for him to finish getting dressed and get out here. It was almost noon, but that's early for guys like Bug. He doesn't hesitate to collect on the sleep he feels he's due. As for me, I'm restless and excited to get the deal rolling. He finally emerged from the front porch, his lanky body still hunched over as if he still needed a good stretch. His thick, pillow-styled hair was sticking out the top of his Haynes T as he pulled it down over his not-so-chiseled abs. As he ambled over to my car, I rolled my eyes, chuckled a bit, and then briefed him on how we'd work this first Fishbowl deal. I moved past the ridiculous notion that he just might need another hour of rest.

We decided to roll in Bug's car since he had been there several times. If we took my ride, it would arouse additional suspicion from the lookouts. Being the new guy in town, I would be scrutinized enough. As we switched cars, I caught myself thinking about the possibilities this operation could present. But as optimistic and hopeful as I was, I could not afford to think that far ahead. I had to focus on now.

When we left, it was around 12:30 p.m. We shot the breeze on the way about everyday things to stay relaxed. It was important to me that we spend time on instruction, details, and planning, but just as important was the need to stay calm and natural. Once we got within minutes of the Bowl, I called my team to make sure they were ready and could hear me over the cell phone connection. Now, it was time to get serious.

My goal was just to get in there, get someone to sell to me, and get out. This would set up my future deals by allowing me to drop a name or to be recognized as at least having been there before.

We entered the neighborhood from the south. Of the two heavily monitored and guarded entrances, this would be the quickest route to the target. We turned in, noting the lookout, and immediately came to a T-intersection - a distinct layout advantage for the bad guys. We hung a right and rounded the corner as I nodded to the sentry on his cell phone. He was already calling ahead. Bug pulled to the curb just past an abandoned, dilapidated house at the northwest corner of Belzise Terrace and Talton Street. From the front passenger seat, I could see about four gangbangers just to the north of us in a vacant lot. They were dressed in baggy jeans, tatted to the nines, and sported the standard Crip blue and orange. As I began to signal them to come to the car, Bug spotted a familiar Firebird.

"Hold up, Tee! I think that's Tre's girlfriend in the Firebird."

"Are you sure, man? Think we can make a little convo?"

"Damn sure gonna try," Bug exclaimed enthusiastically.

I must admit that though I was optimistic, I didn't expect such a lucky break so soon. Tre was a direct descendant of the Douglas family and controlled the south side of the dope business in the Fishbowl. He had been "down" (to prison) a few times on narcotics trafficking, theft, and assault charges. He was rumored to be involved in several shootings. Most recently, he, along with two Crip cohorts, jumped out on a few Bloods and opened fire, but both of the Bloods managed to escape and survive. This would certainly mean Tre would be on edge that much more, so I would have to be particularly careful. This could be a huge break to nab one of my upper-echelon targets if I could work this the right way.

We pulled slightly forward and flagged the Firebird down. As the driver parked the car and approached, the gangbangers from the lot formed a loose circle around us and looked around for cops. The driver of the Firebird was indeed female as she slowly got out and walked right up to my window. She squinted one eye and slowly peered inside with much-expected suspicion. She looked to be about 5-foot-2 and all of 100 pounds, with tattoos exposed about her skimpy tank top and mini skirt. She had a look I can only describe as pretty but worn, if that makes any sense. She acknowledged Bug with a simple nod. But having only seen him before and not me, she was very cautious.

"I heard Tre's girl drives that Firebird," I said.

"Yeah, well, maybe I'm Tre's girl."

"I'm Tee, and this is Bug."

"Candy," she responded suspiciously, then paused. "Is you the po-lice?"

Now, this is one of those times when Hollywood action movies have worked to my advantage. Bad guys in those flicks imply that if you ask an undercover cop if he is the police, he is bound by law to answer you truthfully. I love this because this idea is not only wrong but since she doesn't know that I'll make a little headway with her when I assure her, I am certainly *not* the police.

"Hail, no," I said, "but I was just about to ask you that same question. You just don't see pretty ladies out slingin' "work" (dope to resell) too often. You really with Tre? I've been burned before, and I ain't lookin' for no trouble." I blasted her with counter-questioning to keep her off-balance.

"Shit, you ain't gotta worry 'bout me. Everybody here knows me," she said.

I told her that Bug "hustled" (sold dope) for me, that I was scoring some work for him, and that he had asked me to come along because he said this might eventually be a good spot where I could score.

She proceeded to ask me where I was from, why she hadn't seen me around before, how I knew Bug, and whose car we were in. Typically, I don't tolerate shakedowns, but it seemed as though the more questions she asked, the more the questions seemed to become part of a casual conversation as opposed to an inquisition. I dropped Rabbit's name and avoided details in my answers. Anytime you get too detailed, you appear to be trying too hard. Even worse, you could trip yourself up in a lie.

Finally, I told her we needed to score some "hard" (crack cocaine) for Bug. She was still suspicious but asked me how much I wanted. I told her I wanted nothing but to get Bug what he needed for now. Like any other experienced player walking into a new deal with new dealers, I passed the deal to him. I told her if everything went well, I would return. This kept me from appearing too anxious and solidified my purported suspicion of her.

"Wait here," she said as she went across the street and into an older, refurbished house on the corner with the "hood-standard" chain-link fence in the front. I also noticed several bullet holes in the siding, which would not be considered standard exterior decoration anywhere else but here.

While we waited, I eyed the bangers around our car. I needed them to see me so they would later recognize me, but I didn't want them to see me staring back at them. I put on my sunglasses and watched them in the side-view mirror. When you check your surroundings in a deal like this, you are forced to use creative ways to observe, such as mirrors, car reflections, or window reflections. I watched one particular guy, who seemed to be trying to quietly communicate with the others as he made his way around our car's rear. Bug and I glanced at each other and confirmed we saw the same thing. I was at the ready for a robbery at this point. The guy lifted his t-shirt just enough to expose a silver semi-automatic pistol tucked into his pants. No time for waiting – I reacted. I threw my hands into the air, turned around, looked out the window at him angrily, and exclaimed, "What's up?" I heard Bug utter "Oh, no" under his breath. Usually, it was Bug acting foolish while I shook my head, but not this time. Bug got particularly nervous because he was unarmed, but those are the rules of this game. Besides, Bug is a convicted felon and wouldn't be allowed to carry a firearm even if he wasn't my informant. This move was necessary, though. I had to let these guys know I was not a pushover. Besides, what kind of "big-time dope dealer" lets people intimidate and disrespect him like this, anyway?

No sooner had I reacted than this guy pulled the gun, set it next to his side, and started in toward my window, asking, "Want some of this?" "Whatever, fool," I said as I rolled my eyes and used the opportunity to scan the others around me. I unsheathed my revolver from under my leg and laid it on my thigh, still out of their sight but now at the ready. One of the guys standing in front of our car raised an open hand up to his partner as if to tell him to stop, then said, "It's cool, put that shit up!" He must have seen the potential profits in me.

He had just nipped a potential bloodbath in the bud, too. He smirked, put his gun away, and walked off. I just sighed, rolled my eyes, and set my pistol between my legs - just in case. I turned and looked at Bug. He had been staring at me for a solid minute now with that look in his eye, a look that said, "You son of a bitch. You just scared the piss out of me, but I'm not going to show it right now."

"I got your back, bro," I quietly assured him.

I calmly got out of the car and hollered to the biggest guy there, "Say, I ain't lookin' for trouble here, man. We are just tryin' to get a little work done. This is how business runs in this hood?" I asked.

"Naw, dude, we're straight. Get this done. He's just showin' off anyway."

I knew neither of us needed it to go south this early. That was for sure.

Just then, Candy came back out of the house. I thought I was going to choke on my spit. I see, walking directly behind her, a tall, dark-skinned, 220-pound gangbanger with a long "Ben Wallace" afro sticking straight up in the air. He was cut, tatted from head to toe, and wearing Dickey pants and tennis shoes with no shirt. It was Tre. They walked up and leaned in Bug's window as we introduced ourselves. I was shocked that he had come out, but I knew we were being scoped. Candy needed a second opinion.

Tre motioned for Candy to get the money. Candy walked around to my window, and I gave her my money. I instructed her to hand the dope to Bug. She knew the game. If he worked for me, then he was the one who'd move the stuff. After she handed it over, we examined it closely and suspiciously. I asked her for a weight.

"It's straight-drop," Tre snapped.

Straight-drop is cocaine that is cooked into crack without using any cut or additive to increase the bulk and weight. This was a preference on the street for users since the high was even more intense. But it was a rarity because it was also expensive for the dealer. In other words, Tre had the good stuff, so the weight was less important.

"OK then, we're straight," I told him. "If it really is drop, I'm sure I'll be rolling through again." We pulled away from the curb in utter disbelief that this deal had been such a success.

I looked at it as a test for both of us. I could now holler at Candy for more business if the dope was good. As Bug drove us away, I was grinning ear-to-ear.

"What'cha thinkin' about, Tee?"

"I'm thinkin' we are some lucky fools. You ready to turn over the next card?"

Bug just grinned.

Operation Fishbowl was underway.

I began making solo trips to the Bowl immediately – later that night, in fact. I drove through and asked for Candy, knowing she was likely out since her car was gone. This gave me face time with the sellers there.

"Tell her Tee stopped back by again. I'll catch up to her tomorrow."

They'd look at me suspiciously, but I stayed calm and confident. The more familiar I became, the better my chances would be when I pushed the envelope.

Within days, I received a phone call from an officer who had patrolled the Fishbowl. He was one of the few souls aware I was operating down there – because I trusted him. He was anxious to tell me a couple of outsiders – white guys – had driven into the famous Fishbowl to try to buy dope. They were not regulars. The bangers selling to the guys suspected they were snitching to the police.

So, the bangers surrounded the two, yanked them from the car, beat them with two-by-fours, and left them for dead.

Note to self: Stay focused and alert. And I need to make some more friends.

I'd found an excellent source for friendly intel at a carwash near the Bowl. I always drove through and tipped big with my personal money for guys to wash and detail my ride. It was a fairly dangerous spot, and guys were constantly getting arrested for dealing there, but I just wanted a clean ride and good intel. Over time, a guy named Ced became my regular detailer. Whenever I'd pull in, he'd jump in front of everyone and get me set.

Ced was a Crip but a very personable one. He had a theft and robbery record and a crack addiction. I really liked him.

For one thing, he knew everybody. He didn't move a lot of weight, but he put buyers and sellers together like no one else. He introduced me to a bunch of dealers after a while. We would go cruise the hood and talk about TCU chicks while he hit up a few dealers for me to meet and do a little business. It was as if he was my confidential informant, but I didn't know it. I genuinely liked Ced. He would beg me for my TCU ballcap I wore while we drove around. I teased him about it for a while, but I finally relented and gave him the one my wife had just bought me for my birthday. That would take some explaining, but she'd be cool. It was for the cause. And my cause needed help.

At first, the sellers that Ced connected me with were mid-level street guys and family in the biz just on the perimeter of the Bowl. I soon felt comfortable enough to let Ced know I was eager to ramp up this operation and threw him some extra green to be the man who got me there.

"Well, I can tell you if you wanna big hookup," Ced said. "I know these fools that bring Phat his shit, but they from Poly." Poly was a Crip-ridden eastside neighborhood a mile east of the Fishbowl. I knew it well. It was where I used to run most of my search warrants in Weed and Seed. "X-Man and a dude called Nasty. They huge money. You know who I'm talkin' bout?"

Did I know? I nearly wrecked my ride when I heard the names. That ballcap was paying off already.

CHAPTER 6
"Sunday Morning Drives…
In a Benz"

Every time I went down into the Bowl, I became more familiar to the sellers running each block. If someone down there didn't know me and was overly suspicious, I would simply name-drop or tell him I was taking my business somewhere else. I never tried to push the issue. That's what a cop would do. I stayed decidedly patient. When it came to making money, these guys were going out of their way to be stupid. At worst, they would have me sit tight while they called around and verified if anyone else knew me, and of course, they did. It was getting easier and easier to drive out with evidence of dealing guns or dope on these confirmed gang members.

I still rode with Bug, too. It got to the point where I would bring him along to introduce him to the guys I dealt with. It was important to have him down there, cutting it up with these guys while I was out and vice-versa. This kept me on their minds at all times of the day and night. Bug and I covered every day of the week down there. I even went on weekends to ask for someone I knew to be gone as an excuse to hang around and get to know new bad guys.

Summer nights are hot in Texas, and sharing 40s (the hood's malt liquor size of choice) was the norm. I'd shoot down the blocks with a cold six-pack of Magnum to share and chill. The guys were all over it. I couldn't do the same as easily during the day, though. With so many cops around, me hangin' in the open with these fools would draw unwanted attention. But under the cover of darkness, we bonded.

Sometimes they'd wanna just go rolling with me. See, I'd just procured my own Gangster-Ride: the Mercedes E-Class, previously owned by an eclectic meth dealer who was arrested following a car chase dressed in nothing but a leopard Speedo. Inside, they found a few pounds of meth and guns. He was done – and certainly wouldn't need his ride any longer! It took a lot of string-pulling and red tape, but I finally snagged the Benz and, yes – scrubbed it top to bottom.

Either way, most of the dudes from the Bowl loved my ride. We'd drive around, plow 40s, stop and talk to women or whoever was hanging out slingin' dope in the area. I was beginning to enjoy this time and began to like the guys I was getting to know. There was very little pressure on them when I was not doing business. I recognized that some were, in so many ways, like me. Not the gangbanger aspects of course, but some of these cats were otherwise really good peeps. My perspective grew.

Over the next few weeks, Tre started having me hit his direct cell number for deals. He felt uncomfortable with me driving down there in the Benz all the time – being white was bad enough. I stood out for sure. After that, I'd buzz him, and he'd drive out to meet me wherever. I was in with the big fish.

But now that I had Tre on the hook, I needed to wade my way into the north blocks to make that case on Phat and then get into Poly. Since Ced told me Phat was getting his supply through X-Man, I knew I'd have to make that switch somehow. The difficulty would be moving from one supplier to another without having a good reason. It would be a dangerous but necessary move.

Phat was running a tight ship. He ruled with an iron fist and somehow kept a fairly clean criminal record. He was smart. LP, a Crip from the Fishbowl, had trained him in the ways of gang life and selling dope. LP ran most of the game after the Douglas family was hit a decade earlier. But he ended up shot in a drive-by and was now relegated to a wheelchair. LP stayed in the game but could not maintain the clout he once had. He passed much of his knowledge about the game to Phat, who had expanded on it. With Phat's clean record, he obtained weapons to distribute to other gang bangers when hits were called. He spoke fluent Crab, a Crip dialect that is hard for normal English speakers (or cops) to understand and had a reputation as a skilled street fighter. He'd proven himself by beating on just about whomever he pleased, including two cops. He also ruled the backyard barbeque parties at LPs, where they regularly held crude boxing matches out back.

Very few actually saw Phat handling dope. He had workers servicing the daily customers who purchased guns or the large amounts of crack and marijuana he moved. One of the select few to witness Phat's business from behind the scenes was a guy they called JJ. JJ was a close friend of Phat's, who lived down the street from Phat's supply house in the Bowl. JJ helped Phat distribute his stuff on the street and stashed birds (kilos of cocaine) in his backyard for him. I knew JJ because he liked to hustle dope on the blocks, and I had made a few small-time buys from him during my recent treks. I wanted to use JJ to move up to Phat but had been unsuccessful. JJ seemed to avoid moving me up for fear he would lose me by cutting himself out as the middleman. He would make less money, which was true. Phat and JJ were longtime friends. Though in what I can only imagine was a product of his environment and self-centered lifestyle, Phat added JJ's 14-year-old stepdaughter to his growing list of female conquests as thanks for the work JJ did for him.

When I discovered this during one of our 40-ounce forays, I thought, surely, there would be some falling out between them. But quite a few people I heard talking about it were already aware, and no one confronted Phat, not even JJ. I'm not sure they even thought it was that extraordinary. The power Phat wielded, combined with the need to keep money flowing in the Fishbowl, far outweighed the need for someone to step up in defense of some expendable 14-year-old girl. The sad truth is that the cycle continues to grow, claiming new victims like JJ's stepdaughter every day in hoods and suburbs alike. The cycle stops only when the perps are locked away.

Outside of JJ, Phat had two primary workers who oversaw his business in the street. One of those guys went by the name Cuda. He was a 6-foot, light-complexioned dude with a thick build, short fro, and only a moderate number of tatts. Cuda's job was to ensure that the customers coming into the Fishbowl were buying product evenly between Tre and Phat. Cuda lived with Tre in a house paid for by Phat in the Bowl at the corner of Belsize and Talton – the southernmost block. He had just been released from an eight-year prison stint after having his parole revoked a few years prior. Ironically, his sentence was for delivery of cocaine. Even more ironic was that the last time he had been arrested, it was by me – in uniform! I would only later discover this fact. Thankfully, neither of us would be smart enough to recognize the other until then.

It was an early summer afternoon in 2005 and I was on my way to the Bowl to shoot the breeze with Tre about some future deals. I'd been really burning it at both ends for months now and was feeling it. I was fairly certain my ass was covered, but I also hoped for reasonable success in progressing up the ranks in this op. That meant pushing on and ignoring the lack of sleep or family time. I used others as my motivation for pushing my way onward. As long as I based my hope on making a positive impact on the lives of others, I knew I was at least justified to proceed. If I'd ever begun to make this adventure about personal gain, I think I'd have been on my own. I really did feel OK. The stress and lack of sleep that had set into my everyday life, I knew, was a part of the game I was in. I had to barrel through my days hyper focused, capable and energized. It had to end at some point, but I still had a long way to go.

As I started to pull to my spot on Belzise and Talton, I spotted Cuda walking away. I decided to pull up alongside him in the Benz.

Cuda eyed the car and then saw me. "Damn, you scared me, man. I ain't seen you down here in this ride before. When I first saw the car, I thought you was lost." Since I'd been dealing with Tre remotely, Cuda hadn't really seen me in the baller ride.

"Yeah, I'm not lookin' to get robbed or nothing,' but my other ride's in the shop. I need to score something pretty quick so I can get outta here."

"You right, man. Say, you mess with Tre though, right?"

"Yeah, but I don't think he's home, and I need to get somethin' done now," I told him.

"OK, I'll hook you up, bro. I'm re-upping (refilling his supply) now, anyway. Make the block and meet me back here in 2."

Cuda had recognized me for being around the neighborhood so often, but we had yet to do any business together. This was my prime opportunity for both of us because he knew I'd be easy money, and I knew he'd get me close to Phat. Another problem I'd face was that Phat cooked terrible dope, especially when compared to Tre's straight drop. I'd have to complain about it eventually, but I would worry about that later. I was just excited to see if this opportunity would pan out.

As Cuda walked off, I bought some time by pretending to count my money and watched him as he went straight to the one place that I hoped he would: Phat's house. He went to the front, met with Phat, grabbed a sack of coke, and then started back toward my corner. He was still about 200 yards away, so I split and made the block one time. When I returned to the corner, Cuda had just arrived and hopped in the Benz.

"Love this ride, Tee."

"Keep helpin' me make the payments and I'll let you roll in it anytime, brother," I joked.

We talked for a while about business, prison life and the fact that Cuda was getting back on his feet, and then we did the deal. I paid him from my huge wad of cash I carried for show that consisted of big bills on top and a ton of ones in the middle. It's not just about the Benjamins with me. It's just as much about the Washingtons inside the fold. It was the impression that counted. I just hoped not to be robbed for it.

After scoring from Cuda, I started hitting him up regularly. We got along very well. He was not so out of control as some of the rest. During a visit with the north block dealers one day, I even overheard Cuda had a law enforcement contact giving him and others inside information. Word was this source saved the guys in the Fishbowl several times back in the day by warning them of upcoming task force raids. The hair on the back of my neck stood up as I heard the conversation unfold. Were they about to call me out? This is the stuff that gets UCs like me killed. Once I realized they were not interested in turning their attention toward me, I got pissed. I was determined to get to the bottom of this. If there was really a dirty cop operating down here feeding the bad guys with police intel, I had to get to them before they got to me.

I never share much information if I don't have to because you never know when something like this might happen. I had been making undercover buys in the Fishbowl for several months by this time and had yet to make a formal report. I wrote all my notes on an inter-office form or on napkins in my ride and kept it all hidden at home. Some considered me paranoid, but the bangers in the Bowl I dealt with were capable of anything if I was made. Sgt. Wilson, still my supervisor at the time, understood the magnitude of this operation and the potential for my death if discovered and allowed me to maintain records in this unconventional fashion. I was nearly 100 percent independent but checked in with Wilson daily as a courtesy and to maintain his confidence in me. The rest of my narc team just considered me a rogue, a cowboy. A few of the ignorant ones even figured I was blowing off my duties to go "hang out" somewhere instead of working. I didn't care. Haters will be haters. The right people knew I was busting my balls, and that's all that mattered.

I decided to see Cuda about his " source " in late May of 2005. I called him first and set up a time to meet. I picked him up in the Benz, and we rolled. I told him I was feeling heat on some houses I supplied with coke and "X" (Ecstasy) on the west side and heard he might have a source that could help me get the cops off my back.

"There's a prostitute I know that also cuts hair," Cuda said. "She does this fool called Big Mask's hair. He's supposed to be ex-Task Force, but he's with the Feds or sumthin' now."

"Dude! What'll it cost me, man? I could so use a hook-up like that!"

"Won't cost you nothin,' Tee. Just gimme the addresses you need help with and bring some of that 'X' you movin' by here some weekend and I'll score some from you."

"You're a lifesaver, man," I told him as I dropped him back down into the Bowl.

My mind was racing. I put together a list of addresses and a plan of action to deal with Cuda's source, but before I could get it off the ground, Cuda, that bastard, was arrested again for failing a urine test. He was sentenced to 90 days in a lockdown rehab center run by the Texas prison system. F-ed again.

When he was finally released, I was riding around with Bug and got a call. It was Cuda. The very first call he made out of lockdown was to me. He said he wanted to do business again and said he was relocating to the west side. I asked him about his source that had the police intel again, and he told me he had not been in touch with the chick and didn't think he could contact her. Without his connection to Big Mask, I was unable to justify doing more business with him financially. I had come up in the world and would burn my new contacts if I broke off and dealt with someone else again. He was disappointed and attempted to call me several more times before finally giving up on my money. That lead was dead.

When I hung up the phone, I felt Bug staring at me again from my passenger seat.

"You son of a bitch!" he said, laughing. He hasn't even called me yet, and you're the damn cop! That's unbelievable!"

It was funny, but it also gave me more confidence about the way I was handling myself with these fools. Bug was right. Cuda called me before even calling his own family. He had told me so himself. Tee was actually becoming family to some down here. I was often vouched for by guys who called me "kinfolk." I had to keep the fires burning without burning myself out. And I had to find a roundabout way to nail that son of a bitch police snitch feeding info to these guys from within before I got killed because of it.

With Big Mask now a grave concern, I was stressed more than ever. I started this operation by myself, but I had never felt this alone. I was spending 60 hours a week on the clock and another 30 hours working OTB ops. It was me against the world and in my mind, I began to really live this game. I wanted to win it, but I got the feeling I needed to be careful, or I would begin to forget who I was.

CHAPTER 7
"A Window of Opportunity"

Leaving for my real home from a gang scene that I'd just been involved in proved to be a little unnerving after time. I'd hinted to these dudes where I lived but always gave a general area in lieu of a specific spot. Real dealers would do the same. After all, I was here to do business, not share my life.

Making "heat runs" became commonplace. To make a heat run means to drive away in a specific direction, check your six for anyone or anything behind you, and then intentionally make your way back to your original locale. If someone is following you, they will either be "made" by ending up in the same place, and you deal with them accordingly, or they are forced to bail when they realize you are headed straight back to your original spot, which allows you to then split - sans the caboose.

Ced and I had been hanging out, and it was late. We were east of the Fishbowl in Poly, where there was much for me to do. I had made some serious progress to this point, but still managed to miss X-Man. But I had dodged certain demise, and now, with so much on the line, I was chilling comfortably with 'ole Ced. After a 40-ounce and a dominating performance of Madden on X-Box, I decided it was time to split.

"I'm out, fool. My girl is gonna wonder where I am," I told him.

"No way, Tee! You can't leave until I get another chance to whoop your ass at this game."

"Ain't gonna happen because I'd be here all night beating you down while you try to con me into another double-or-nothin! Besides, if you were handsome enough that a girl would consider wondering where you were, you'd split too."

"Ahh man, fuck you!" he said jokingly, but defeated.

I tossed him the other two 40s I had with me and headed out. I scanned the porch into the street and peered out the corner of my eyes as I approached my car to be certain no one would surprise me. When I got into the car and locked the doors, I called my bro who'd been standing by in his patrol car while I partied and told him he could split because I was done for the night. He'd been in a patrol car about five blocks away, listening to me on his phone. It was almost impossible to make out exactly what was being said, but he knew I would speak up if something went sideways, and he had to crash through the locked door and extract me. That is still something I certainly did not want since it would blow my cover for good. And I wasn't done.

I took off and began my heat run alone. No cops. No bad guys. No problems. I was in the clear and on my way home. Hitting the freeway, I decided to open it up. Windows down, tunes blaring, and the cool night sky smiled upon me. Things were looking back up indeed. Or were they? I should have checked the trunk for Murphy (of Murphy's Law), I thought to myself.

Ever have those moments where you suddenly realize that you are enjoying yourself just a little too much for your own good, and that fate was sure to counter your growing ego? Tonight would be that night. The freeway noise was a little much, so I rolled my windows back up. I exited early and would take a backway home tonight. Mixing up my routes was another way to preserve my anonymity…and my life. The stereo played my typical "mood music," which combined my taste for funk, soul, rock & roll, and the hood's current rap styles. This time, The Roots were crunk. The tune "Step Into The Realm" cut the air and enhanced the natural high of temporary success I enjoyed. The lyrics chanted as the backbeat took precedence:

"Step into the realm; you're bound to get caught, and from this worldly life, you'll soon depart." I should have been listening more attentively.

Guns had become a recurring theme in this case. More thugs had threatened to shoot me in the past year than had previously in my whole life. The advantage, if there is such a thing, to having a gun presented against you is that you can assess your next move and, in cases of trained folks, remain in some control. The one situation I hadn't considered to this point was dealing with the gun you don't see. All these fools carried. I knew they did, and they knew I did. However, I neglected to consider one of the most cowardly ways gangs deal with an enemy – the drive-by.

Drive-by shootings illustrate the underlying carelessness that exists in many of these guys—most of whom are simply looking for opportunities to belong and be respected. Over the years, gangs have used the drive-by to invoke fear and to show power, never considering the collateral damage that is often caused by shooting innocents in the process or by avoiding a proper man-to-man method of conflict resolution. It is all a part of the sociopathic way in which gangs have evolved, and now it seems to be the simple standard. Having chilled with these guys so much to this point, I knew they had some common sense and, in many cases, even a truly sympathetic heart. If they could only see these shootings from the opposing family's perspective, see the aftermath that befalls a mother after seeing her son die, then perhaps they would understand. Perhaps. This is the perspective we cops are most used to seeing. Now that I see the other side, it only pains me more to know that this still goes on despite neither side truly understanding what destruction they are putting into motion. All the bangers I know with a heart need their peers to lead them away from this puss tactic, and they'd gladly refrain. Followers will be followers, though.

Once, back in my patrol days, having just finished a weightlifting session during my "lunch break" (Although 3 a.m. can only be considered lunch for the select few working nightshifts), a "shots fired" call went out on Avenue G in Poly. It was my beat, so I was determined to get there first...and I did. As I pulled up to the house about three doors down and blacked my cruiser out, I called in my arrival to dispatch.

"George 3-15 (my unit identifier at the time), 10-23 (on the scene). Standing by."

"Copy George 3-15."

I scanned the immediate area to see if anyone was still outside or still firing rounds. The house was dark, as was the street surrounding it. There was a vacant lot adjacent to the house that I'd have to remain cognizant of as I calculated my next move. I noticed a chain-link fence around the front yard, but the gate was open toward me as if the last person utilizing it was on their way out. Noted. The smell of gunpowder emitted from the dark scene, and I knew what I had to do. To potentially preserve lives in this exigent circumstance, I couldn't afford to wait for backup to arrive. I tactically approached the target residence, avoiding windows with a line of sight, and noticed the front door was slightly open. I radioed dispatch again – quietly.

"George 3-15, close the [radio] channel. I have an open door at the target residence. Keep my 63s (backup) coming. I'm going in."

"George 3-15, we are clear. George 13 and 16 are enroute to your location. All units, be advised that this channel is closed," the dispatcher responded.

It was pitch black and eerily quiet. I positioned my tactical flashlight and my Sig-Saur .40-cal to allow me to clear rooms efficiently, all the while prepared to shoot. I controlled my breathing so as not to be heard until I announced my presence and to ward off some of the inevitable sympathetic nervous system adrenaline dump already in progress. As I pied and cleared the first room through the front door (scanned sections of a room like a pie in sequence while using cover or concealment), I shouted my announcement as I quickly entered.

"Fort Worth Police! Come out and let me see your hands!"

I then began to pie and clear areas rapidly. As I button-hooked or crossed doorways, I brought my weapon close to my chest to keep a perp around a corner from accessing it and then would quickly re-extend the weapon once I cleared the threshold so I could more accurately and expeditiously launch rounds.

I made my way down a smoky, dark hallway and noticed the distinct illumination and faint sound of a television coming from a rear living room. I made my announcement again to be sure that whoever was there knew I was no foe. I hurried to the doorway edge, pieing the room as I entered. Then, I came upon a horrific sight. There I was, inside the darkest house in the hood, the smell of freshly fired ammunition filling my senses while scurrying through the place to keep from being shot and potentially save a life. And there he was, the victim, with his X-Box pro wrestling game still running – round timer and everything. He had been shot dead – straight through the eyeball. This had just happened, too. The video game timer told me so.

I rapidly cleared the remainder of the small frame house to ensure no perps or additional victims existed. All else was clear.

"George 3-15, I have a signal 12 (deceased person) here. No other suspects or victims on scene. Slow my 63s and notify Homicide."

The experience was spooky but also intriguing. There were bullet holes everywhere. After we cordoned off the crime scene and Homicide detectives began prodding about and measuring bullet trajectories, they determined that the vast majority of the shots came from inside the house. The theory that resulted from their subsequent investigation of the scene was that there were three gang members in this house – Crips. The guys inside heard what they thought to be shots fired from outside and immediately assumed they were in the middle of a drive-by shooting. Guns were pulled and shots rang out from inside. Apparently, one of these fools was not so gun savvy, and as he drew his weapon from the back of his pants and raised it toward the window, a round accidentally launched into the eye of his homeboy, who had not yet begun to move away from his video game, killing him instantly. The panicking Crips then decided to empty all their rounds outside to mimic what they would claim was a gun battle with Bloods outside. Then they just hauled ass. And I just missed them. I was pissed.

This is my lasting firsthand impression of what a drive-by represents. Random death sentences bestowed onto people often only remotely related to someone they hate that they cowardly decide to attack. I'd worked dozens of drive-bys in my career, but this situation, though not quite a legitimate drive-by, was so spooky and senseless that it stuck firmly in my memory.

I turned down a dark back road and still had my tunes up. There was a smattering of small businesses on my left and a lower-to-middle-class neighborhood on my right. By this time, I was more than halfway home and about 10 minutes away from the Fishbowl area. I was relaxed…and letting my guard down.

Suddenly, a loud gunshot rang out as my rear passenger window shattered from the neighborhood side! I swerved, ducked, and immediately pulled across the street behind a business for cover. I turned off my stereo and darked out. My breathing and heart rate increased as I tried to quickly understand what had just happened. Then, the idiot in me surfaced. I pulled my 5-shot revolver from under my leg, flipped my headlights back on, and screeched back out onto the street and immediately into the neighborhood from which the shot rang. I lowered my front passenger-side window, the one that had survived the shooting, and held my gun firmly as I pointed it out, ready to shoot the perpetrator (as if that were even practical!).

I searched everywhere, screaming for the shooter to show himself and that I was going to kill the son of a bitch. It was not the smartest thing I had ever done, but after the initial shock of the fact that I'd been shot at passed, I became enraged. Up and down the streets, I raced. Screaming and aiming the best I could. I searched until I realized that no one was going to surface. I'd been a victim of a drive-by miss. What's worse, I had been paying so little attention that I had no earthly idea who it was or where it came from. After thinking about it, I knew there was no way the shot came from a house in the neighborhood. There was no way someone could have predicted my arrival there, let alone taken an accurate shot as I passed randomly. I had to have been shot at by a vehicle, which was way worse. Someone was following me. I'd led them halfway to my real home, and I could not let that ever happen again! After my heat run, I had stopped paying close enough attention to protect myself or even my family in this case. From this point on it would take me 50 minutes to arrive home from the hood that was a mere 20 minutes away.

Now, my secondary concern was the mystery of the whole event. I had no idea who could have done this. I had to either react swiftly and harshly or treat it as if it were another day at the office. Since I hadn't a lead to go on, making a scene would weaken my position with the bangers I had no issues with. So, I elected to go with the latter. Other than figuring out how to explain my vehicle damage, I'd treat this like any other day.

In that regard, the only advantageous thing I'd done that night was actually something I didn't do. I never called this in or asked for backup. I was so used to working alone that it had not even occurred to me by this point. This allowed me time to figure out how to get my car repaired without disclosing the fact I'd been shot at. I pondered a strategy. I would never lie to Wilson, who'd given me so much rope because of our trust. But if I told him that I had been shot at on my way home from chilling with a bunch of bangers I'd targeted without a cover team, he'd certainly shut me down, and Operation Fishbowl would screech to a devastating halt.

I marched into his office the next morning, fighting off a nervous smile. "Hey, Sarge – might need you to come to scope a booboo on my ride if you have a sec." His eyes rolled toward the ceiling, and he let out a long sigh as if to prepare himself. Without a word, he stood up and followed me to my ride, which I'd parked in a secret and secured rear lot at the Narc office.

"Well, here it is, boss."

"I can't wait for this one," Wilson said enthusiastically. He stood right beside the Benz, hands on hips, fixated on the shattered rear passenger window.

That is when I half-confidently floated my certain truth. "Sarge, isn't it so hard to believe an errant rock could do this much damage to a side window?"

He looked ever-so-slowly up to the sky and paused. The awkward silence seemed to last forever, but I waited patiently in anticipation of a real ass-chewing. Then, in an act of defeated concession, he slowly turned around and walked back toward his office.

"Yes, Tegan. It is very hard to believe."

I love Sergeant Wilson.

CHAPTER 8
"Finding Pino"

2004: The deal with "Killer-B" was set. It was a short-term project to nail this dealer who'd been responsible for several complaints from the neighborhood. I'd get this buy, write a warrant, kick his door in, and take him to jail. This was routine. I picked up my informant and cruised to Killer-B's apartment. As we pulled up, the traffic jammed. Crowds had gathered up and down the street, and emergency vehicles were leaving the scene. I told my informant to see what the ruckus was about while I parked. Obviously, we couldn't work with all these cops around. Within minutes, he sprinted back over to me with a look of surprised shock on his face.

"You'll never believe it, bro! Killer-B's gone!"

"Well, you know, that ain't weird. These fools live by their clock and their clock only. Besides, we can't do business here tonight anyway. I'll call him tomorrow and tell him he missed out on some business."

"Na man, you don't get it. Some dudes robbed his ass and killed him!"

I paused. Stuff like this hit home with me. This is a business that cares for no one, including me. People in the game pretend they are loyal, insist on being respected, and want you to trust them. But the reality is that this game stops for no one, and the people in it are foolish to think they are actually trusted, respected, or loyal. In fact, recruiting someone into a gang to run dope is one of the more disingenuous things one can do to another. There are only false promises, betrayal, fear, addiction, and the façade of love that is always breached. This illustrates my point to a T. People grieve for a minute, then return to their precious game until the next casualty hits.

In an incredible twist of irony, the next year, my wife Holli and I were helping a needy family at Christmas. This family had become close to us and though they didn't have much, they also learned to give to others. While visiting, we noticed an extra kid playing around the house. He was a cool little dude, about four years old then. We decided to buy a few toys for him and the others since he was there so often. His name was Cedric, and he stayed there so frequently because his mother was an addict and his father had recently been killed. When I learned he was actually Killer-B's son, I was shocked. This kid was going to need love and attention. I was proud of our friends for giving it. The serendipity of this whole scenario will stay with me.

After Cuda was arrested in 2005, I was still buying in the Bowl from Tre but also from other violent bangers, young and old. One scorching mid-July day in 2005, without calling ahead, I rolled into the Bowl unexpectedly and asked the guys on the south blocks to go get Tre. While I waited, I hung out with the sellers, talking about business, women, and gang life. They always spoke freely about the gang stuff because I acted (and looked) like I didn't know a thing about it. I scored a yard ($100 worth of crack) from a guy I owed a little favor and then began chatting up a newbie. The guy introduced himself as "Big Stick." Stick had an unassuming appearance. He was about 24, tall, thin, and dark-skinned. Turns out he was a legit gangbanger and a real hustler. I recognized the name and later ran some recent reports naming him a suspect in a couple of shootings. I stretched the conversation and tried to learn as much as I could. I even let him talk me into buying work from him, too. Getting delivery cases would be vital if I wanted violent ones like him put away. I scored a small amount since I was suspicious of new dealers, and I was supposedly doing him a favor. He was fine with that, and so was I – especially with my limited funds.

One of the biggest hurdles I faced was my buy-money budget. I was making so many buys that I was more than tripling the amount my entire team spent weekly. Worse, I was not making any arrests. It didn't look good on paper, but I had the complete trust of Sgt. Wilson, who truly believed in me and in this operation. He would go to bat for me more than was fair. These small buys benefitted me because they allowed me to make multiple cases on bad guys without exhausting my already-exceeded budget.

I was also fortunate to snag a few cases on Stick when I did. In the coming months, Stick would wear out his welcome in the Bowl by robbing dealers and then reselling the stolen dope at a huge discount. This was a major breach of the Bowl rules that Phat set up. You had to get permission from Phat or Tre to sell dope in the Bowl. If you were cool to sell on the blocks, you would be made to sell their dope and pay them a hefty cut for allowing you to sell it. Stick was breaking these rules of the street by bringing in stolen dope and then taking on Fishbowl customers willing to risk their lives to buy at an incredible discount.

At one point, Stick sold Phat's dope, then switched to Tre's dope because Phat's dope was crap. Phat didn't care when Stick switched suppliers, but when he first found out Stick had been bringing in his own dope, he nearly beat the life out of him. To make things worse, while Stick was selling Tre's dope, he decided to rob Tre himself at gunpoint three separate times. He managed to get away with an SKS assault rifle, $3,000 in cash, and a half-kilo of coke in the first robbery. In the second robbery, he got away with more dope and $12,000 cash. The third attempt turned out a bit differently. One of Phat's boys, "D," was there, and he would later recall the incident to me in an interview:

I was sittin' in the living room in the Ash Crescent [Tre's] house. "RayRay" knocks on the door, so I get my pistol and go up there, but I only open the door part, not the bars. Then RayRay asks me where Tre at. I ask him what he wanted. He say he wants work, so I go get the key from the bedroom to let him in. Tre was in his room with Aiesha and baby McCoy asleep. When I let RayRay in, he lets Stick and Wix in with 12-gauge shotguns. Then RayRay pulls out a 9 [mm] and points it at me and makes me get on the ground. Then Tre came out and Stick makes Tre get on the ground. Tre didn't get all the way down at first and Stick told him 'you better get down cuz. I wanna kill you anyway.' Then Wix went to Pacc's room and kicked the door in. Pacc's wife was on the bed, but Pacc was hidin' in the closet. Then Pacc fired a warning shot, then he shot Wix in the neck. Then Wix falls back into the living room. Stick ran his ass out of there and RayRay grabbed Wix and got him out while he was shootin' back at us. That's when he shot me in the back of the leg. I chased him out with my .40 [caliber] and started shootin' at their car. I couldn't run too good, but I was still shootin'.

No one went to the hospital since the gunshot wounds were superficial. The last thing these guys want is for the police to get involved. That way, they can take care of business their way – true street justice. D had a scar on his calf but was fine. Wix, the Crip friend of D's who hung around the Bowl occasionally, walked around with his wounded shoulder permanently shrugged up like he was trying to squash a bug, and RayRay would eventually be arrested for a drive-by that killed a young teen in the Bowl. Not long after the last robbery attempt, I noticed Stick working again in the Bowl for Tre. I was perplexed. Initially, I was told that Stick was making up for Tre's losses by working for him and that the two had made up. I would later learn Tre brought Stick in close so he could kill him when the time was right. Now that made sense!

Before Tre could execute his master plan, Stick ripped a guy for a bird (kilo) and was arrested for transporting it from Texas to Louisiana. He stayed in prison until the day I charged him with my deals. Although this circumstance spared Stick's life, two of Stick's victims would not experience the same fate. I would learn later that Stick wasn't only a robber, a drug dealer, and gangbanger, but he was also a murderer. I'd discover he was responsible for two cold-case murders in Fort Worth. One was the 1998 murder of a transvestite/prostitute, who, at Stick's request, gave him a blow job before discovering the prostitute was actually a male. The other, in the ultimate twist of a twist, was the 2004 robbery and murder of a Fort Worth dope dealer named Killer-B. I would later contact my family friends to inform them that I had managed to put little Cedric's dad's killer behind bars. There was obvious relief and tempered joy that Stick would likely never see daylight again. These stories became stranger than fiction in this case, but as long as the results remained positive, it would all be worth it. Man charged in transvestite slaying:

FORT WORTH — A man already charged in connection with a 2004 slaying now stands accused of fatally shooting a transvestite six years earlier after learning that the victim, with whom he'd had a brief sexual relationship, was not a woman but a man. Iman Johnson, 26, was charged with murder Thursday in connection with the slaying of a 19-year-old victim in Fort Worth.

"The motive appeared to be that he had a previous relationship with the victim, not knowing that the victim was actually a male," said homicide Sgt. J.D. Thornton. "He later found out from some of his friends that [he] wasn't a woman, and then he basically hunted him down and killed him."

A man walking behind the Shop & Stop convenience store in the 2600 block of South Riverside Drive on the night of Sept. 8, 1998, found the body, dressed in women's clothing, a few feet from a sidewalk. He had been shot several times with a shotgun, police have said.

Johnson remains in federal prison in Fort Worth in connection with Operation Fishbowl, a 20-month local and federal investigation of the southeast Fort Worth drug trade that led to 40+ indictments. He was charged with capital murder in February in the robbery and fatal shooting of 24-year-old D'Kevin Anderson. Anderson was gunned down in the 4900 block of Flamingo Road while running from two armed men who went to his apartment on July 25, 2004, and robbed him of drugs and money. A second man, 24-year-old DeShawn Adams, is also charged with capital murder in connection with Anderson's death.

Thornton said it was during Detective Matt Hardy's investigation of the Anderson case that Johnson also surfaced as a suspect in the other murder. "He interviewed several persons, one of which indicated that Johnson was also involved in the murder of a transvestite some years ago," Thornton said. "Hardy was able to locate the case matching the details given by the witness."

It was now the fall of 2005, and I was trying desperately to expand my business, but I felt like I was in a rut. X-Man was beginning to feel like a pipedream. Tre picked up a new partner named "Dank," whom I had been spending lots of time with on the south blocks. Dank was very young, up-and-coming, and wanted badly to be respected as a gangbanger. He was a little dude, around 5-foot-7, 140 pounds, who talked a big game and always carried a gun. But mainly because he was Tre's, no one messed with him.

I began cruising around the hoods with Dank and watching him do business. He was fielding phone calls for Tre and handling orders from various customers. I'd hoped he might eventually get deep enough to connect to Phat later. But I had an even better idea for one of his connects. One notable customer of Dank's was a dude named "Pino." Pino was a guy I'd run across a few times in the Bowl myself. A big 'ole boy, he certainly looked formidable but seemed somehow out of his element – awkward even. Pino had just received a large inheritance and was buying up dope to flip like it was going out of style. He was a small-time hustler before but had blown up since the money rolled in. Pino scored from Tre and Dank but was concerned that he would eventually get jacked. Big or not, these Bowl cats will do your ass in a second if they smell an opportunity. I hit Pino up one day outside Dank's car after a deal while Dank was on a phone call. I'd been waiting for this opportunity. I asked him about his business and shared an idea about how we could reduce the risk of him being set up and enhance each other's game.

Pino was a sole proprietor from Poly – X-Man's turf. He couldn't make much hay in Poly because he grew up there and wasn't claiming a set. They also knew him too well and would take him for his money. He did find a little success with some of the dudes in the Bowl, of course, but was just scared to death that he was gonna get hit, and it would be over like that.

"Here's the deal, P," I told him. "You know I'm established in the Bowl. I got 'peeps' who can and will back my ass up if someone ever tries to mess with me. I'm sure you know this even from the little time you've been down there. How about you make all your buys as my boy like you're picking up work for me. That way, not only would a potential hitter assume you weren't the real moneyman, but they'd also know you were off limits cuz you're with me."

"OK. I'm trackin'. But what's in it for you?" he asked reservedly. "I ain't dumb, ya know."

He wasn't dumb. There is always a trade-off, and as I've said before, the game only cares about the game.

"Yo, I'm getting to that. So, you from Poly. I'm established over here, but I am tryin' to come up –all the way up. Like X-Man status, up. Think you can make me a few intros into Poly so I can expand my enterprise?"

"Shit, easily, Tee. If that's all you need, then we got a deal."

In my mind, this was risky but one of the only ways I could sustain my status as a big-time dope dealer without actually spending much money. And even though Pino wasn't a massive dealer in Poly, he knew those cats intimately. All I needed was a door to crack, and I'd do the rest. Pino, in turn, would also inadvertently feed me updates on my targets as he set deals up on my behalf, earning me even more street cred, and keeping his ass alive with it.

The plan worked. Pino started calling me at all hours of the day and night whenever he planned to pick up dope or gun orders for his customers. He would tell me what he intended to pick up and who he wanted to buy from. Then, I would call the suppliers and tell them what I needed. When it was set, I would tell them I was sending Pino to pick it up. Pino would pick up and pay for his stuff, and everyone thought I was buying like crazy. Now, if only Pino could help me expand toward X-Man. I was playing the patient game.

Pino called. He needed a quarter-kilo of powder cocaine within the hour – the good stuff. I told him I would work something out and call him back. I told Bug it was about time I revisited Tre's house – without friggin' Carlos and without asking the guys on the block to fetch him. Besides, it was daytime, and daytime always felt like a slightly safer time to do business. This would be another OTB op for me. Much of my life by this time had become OTB. I was beginning to feel way more like a hustler than a cop. I came up with a quick plan of action. Bug would go meet with Pino and set up at the meeting place while I went straight to Tre's door and negotiated the dope. It was a power play, but I needed to push limits to see where I stood.

I drove to Tre's house unannounced around noon and parked the Benz at the boarded-up house next door. It had been abandoned for as long as I could remember. It resembled a haunted house, even in the daylight. It had old, rickety boards loosely covering dark windows, doorways, and overgrown weeds that now looked crooked and thick. Add this to the risk of violence at Tre's next door, and it was a ready-made Hollywood horror movie combo. As I crossed the yard from the north and approached the front door, I fought back thoughts of Carlos and remembered that we still left on a positive note. I knocked, hoping for Tre and not the Toothless Wonder-Puss. Tre answered the door.

"Damn, Tee, a surprise visit?"

I played it off casually, ignoring the fact that I was breaking the rules.

"Sorry, I didn't have time to call, bro. I just need to holler at you 'bout some last-minute business. It's just me today, so you won't need any carpet cleaner this time," I half-joked.

Tre let me in without saying another word and locked the burglar bar door behind me. The sound of the creaking bolt forcing its rusty way into the black wrought-iron latch was awakening. I was locked in. I stood in the living room tactically, with my back to the only non-exposed wall and, again, near that door. The memories flowed. I made sure no one could sneak behind me and that I could still see the other areas where a bad guy could attack me. If something went wrong and with no backup, I'd have to kill everyone in there. I knew firsthand that there were often loons in this joint, so I stayed cool.

Tre walked across the living room stoically and sat on the couch against the opposing wall in front of a coffee table. On that table sat two semi-automatic handguns both coincidentally (or perhaps not) pointed toward me. It was like a scene from a mobster movie, as he seemed to lean back onto the couch in slow motion behind those guns, crossed his arms, and asked in his best Pacino:

"What you need?"

"Quarter bird – soft." I was cool.

"By when?"

"Well, that's just it, man. I need it in 30 minutes if you got it. I can cover a little extra green for the short notice."

Just then, his roommate, Pacc, a convicted felon on parole for robbery, came into the room and raised a stainless .45. I immediately pulled the gun from under my shirt before I realized who it was.

"Dang Pacc, you scared me half to death!" I said, without lowering my piece.

"Oh, Tee! How you been, man?"

Pacc put his pistol away into the back of his pants. His pistol was so big he couldn't fit it in the front! I knew Pacc well and had done many deals with him before. He was one of the few guys in the Bowl I counted on to get my back if other fools like Stick tried to rob me. We had talked about it several times. He was old school and had been in the game for longer than some of the other fools on the blocks had been alive. Relieved, I put my pistol away, too. I figured Pacc was making sure it wasn't Stick at the friggin' door trying to rob them again!

"Good to see you, bro. We're just handlin' a few details," I said.

"We straight," Tre told him.

"Good, then I'm goin' back to sleep!"

"Naa, can't go yet, Paccy! Tee needs work."

Pacc returned to the bedroom to get dressed, and Tre told me he could have the quarter in minutes. He wanted $4500 for it. I negotiated for a bit to keep it realistic and then agreed to pay $4300. I just took another big step.

Tre said he and Pacc would meet me and to be ready in 10 minutes. I agreed but had a dilemma: this dope was for Pino, but Tre wanted to bring it to me. If I took the dope, I'd be obligated to seize it – and couldn't resell it. If I seized it, Pino obviously couldn't have it, and here I was, OTB. But I covered this in my genius plan.

Around 12:35, Bug and I, in separate cars, parked at the meeting spot that turned out to be a mall parking lot a few miles from the Bowl. Bug parked to my right and about 20 feet behind me. Pino gave me the money and watched from his car about 100 yards away in an elevated spot with a good view of the deal. Pacc and Tre pulled up in a car I had never seen before. Pacc was driving, and Tre was in the front passenger seat. They pulled up next to my Benz. I saw Pacc hand something over to Tre and then saw Tre shove something into his pants before he came over and got into my car.

He sat down and immediately started pulling something from the front of his pants. I stopped him.

"Hang on. I'll get you in a sec." I looked around as if to watch for the police as I counted out the money for him. I was taking a little control over this deal. I'd picked the spot, and now I was pushing to see if he'd cooperate with my new handoff routine. I handed Tre the money.

"Go see Bug for the rest of the deal, and I appreciate you," I said, pointing to the car behind me. Tre had no problem with this since I would have asked to see the dope first if it were a set-up. Tre got out and disappeared from my view as he got into Bug's car. He supposedly handed the bag of dope to Bug, who tested and weighed it. When he was satisfied, Tre split with Pacc, and Bug met with Pino. The plan went as smoothly as silk. Dope deal: Pino. Credit: Tee.

I was now a big deal in the Fishbowl. I had dodged bullets and actually thought I might be nearing the point that I could stop and arrest all of these violent bastards – if it weren't for the compelling idea that I now might get deep enough to nab X-Man. After all, I had established solid gun and dope cases on nearly 20 key Fishbowl players by this time. I wasn't finished, though. The truth is I wasn't even close to finished, and I would soon discover something that would take me all the way back to the beginning.

CHAPTER 9
"What Jim Henson Never Intended"

I spent hours at night trying to figure out a strategic way to leverage an intro from Pino into Poly, the larger Crip turf only a mile or so east of the Bowl. I toiled over the best targets to start on in search of X-Man's runners to Phat. I should have been sleeping, but sleep was a rarity by this time. I received calls daily from the Bowl players or Pino wanting me to score. Then, one day, I got a call from a friend in patrol who had been on my Weed and Seed teams and had been approached by a guy with information about dope houses. He figured I could best use the information since I worked in Narcotics. The kicker was that this guy claimed he had worked for several dealers in Poly but was getting ripped off. He said now his baby brother was getting deep in the game, and he wanted to get them both out before his life took a turn he could not right.

During my conversation with the officer, I heard enough familiar names to talk to this guy. The officer explained that I was an experienced undercover officer and I'd call him from an unknown number. I called and began talking with him over the phone; I'd let him speak and answer questions about things I already knew to properly verify his info. His street name was Smurf. He was cautious of me, and I was of him initially. Neither of us wanted this to be a mistake. Hell, I may make a little progress here without Pino's slow ass!

My main objective: X-Man. Smurf said he knew him well. Everybody knew of him, but few truly knew him. I became convinced that Smurf at least had a reasonable connection to get to him through a ruthless banger he worked for named Deuce. Years earlier, he had been identified by cops investigating a murder as "Dus," but his tatts read "Deuce." As dangerous a move as it was at this point, I had to take every possible chance to move forward into the next phase of Operation Fishbowl: The Polywood Crips – the home set of X-Man.

Smurf and I eventually met several times outside the neighborhood and discussed who and what he knew and how I planned to work with them. He was motivated to tell the truth since he knew there was no cash or protection from arrest with a sack of lies. Plus, he was also in this to try and separate his brother from the dope game, and I respected that motivation. However, I made it clear in no uncertain terms that a lie or fabrication would end all possibilities for either of them. He seemed to be telling the truth and gave me tons of information I could use. It was nerve-wracking because I couldn't even ask Pino about him or I'd run the risk of others finding out he was an informant, or worse, that I was a cop. Bug knew I was a cop. Now Smurf knew I was a cop. That was already enough to keep me awake at night. Eventually, Smurf and I began to trust one another. I was motivated by what he brought to the table, but I would never cross a line that would get him exposed or killed. Unlike many other cops I knew, I truly cared about my informants as people. Yes, they are most often boneheads. However, the sheer nature of their position was so precarious that my goal was to work with them until I got to know them. Then, I could steer them into a legitimate, achievable vocation where personal success would lead them away from this dead-end game.

Smurf and I began rolling through the Poly hood to become a familiar fixture in the minority-laden landscape. Anytime some new white guy claiming to be somebody rolls through these dealing havens, it raises flags – and heat. I was going to soften the blow of being introduced, by being, at least by sight, familiar.

Smurf eventually told me about a place you could fence just about anything imaginable. He directed me to a warehouse the bad guys worked out of and explained that he had sold a few guns and even a stolen truck there. By this point I knew the guy trusted me, or he wouldn't risk incriminating himself in other crimes he'd recently committed. When I started to investigate this fencing operation to verify the story, I discovered it was a sting operation by our FWPD Property Crimes Unit, which had a warrant for Smurf related to the guns and the truck. At least I knew he wasn't lying!

I had to jump through multiple hoops, planning with the judge for Smurf to work the cases off instead of going to jail – where he'd be useless to me and be in the one place he abhorred. I used the situation to my advantage, though. Not having to pay Smurf for his services would be another way I could still try to be the supposed big-time dope dealer without ever really spending big-time dope money.

FORT WORTH 1997 - An 18-year-old suspect in the slaying of a store clerk this week has an alibi that prevents police from pressing a capital murder case against him, police said yesterday.

"Deuce", of the 2900 block of Bideker Avenue, was being held on suspicion of capital murder in connection with the shooting death of a local store clerk, said Lt. Mark Krey, a police spokesman.

However, Deuce remained in Tarrant County Jail last night, facing a charge of criminal attempted murder in an unrelated case, officials said. Deuce is jailed in lieu of $50,000 bail in connection with the shooting of a 17-year-old on July 30, according to a police report. If police do not file a case with the district attorney's office within 72 hours of a suspect's arrest, the suspect must be released. The case could not be made against Deuce, Krey said. Deuce "provided an alibi, but we haven't been able to prove or disprove it at this point," he said.

No other suspects are in custody in connection with the brazen robbery-slayings Tuesday night and early Wednesday morning by a group of bandanna-clad gunmen. Also, authorities say, the robbers in an early morning holdup of a Winn-Dixie store Thursday closely match the description of the bandits.

In the first robbery, a 33-year-old man from Arlington was slain about 11:40 p.m. Tuesday at the S & A Food Store at 2912 Vaughn Blvd. Police said two men shot and killed the father of five children.

Less than two hours later, the 27-year-old manager of a pool hall on Brentwood Stair Road, was shot once in the back of the head while complying with demands to remove his rings, police said. Physical evidence found at both scenes positively linked the two killings, investigators said. The owner of the pool hall has offered a $5,000 reward for information leading to the conviction of the killers.

Detectives said they believe that the killers and their accomplices belong to a specific gang because of the color and type of clothing witnesses said they wore. Authorities are still searching for three of the four men in those killings. Police said witnesses in the clerk's killing described one of the gunmen has having distinctive hair braids, which matched Deuce's appearance.

About 1:25 a.m. Thursday, three masked gunmen terrorized employees at a grocery store on Meadowbrook Drive shortly after closing. A store manager was pistol-whipped during the robbery. Authorities say they believe that the three crimes might be linked to the same suspects.

"There are some glaring similarities," Homicide Sgt. Paul Kratz said. "However, until we positively identify some of the suspects in the killings, we can't link" the grocery store robbery.

In August of 2005, I decided where I'd launch my Poly buy attempt with Smurf – Deuce. Deuce was a friend, a dedicated gangster, and an X-Man business associate. He transported, cooked, and sold X-Man's dope by setting up residences and placing trusted personnel inside to do the daily hand-to-hand transactions. Deuce had an extremely menacing look for a guy with such a name. He was 6-foot-1, 220 pounds, dark-skinned with braided hair and gang tatts everywhere. Deuce was a ruthless gangbanger who was very proud of his Crip affiliation. He was an original member of a set of Crips led by X-Man called the Polywood Crips. Deuce ran Bideker Street, which was in Poly. It was as if he were the operations manager for that area. He had an incredibly violent history, beginning when he was a teen. At that time, he and X-Man decided to rob a food store in the center of Poly. X-Man drove the getaway car and watched the parking lot while Deuce covered his face with a blue bandana, went inside the popular store, and did the robbery. As Deuce ran out of the store with the take, the clerk cussed at him. Deuce, feeling disrespected, shot and killed the clerk on the spot. After they escaped the scene, Deuce went to Smurf and made him get rid of the gun. He was arrested then, but there wasn't enough evidence for a conviction. I was becoming privy to a lot of this very helpful inside info. It felt good to be on the inside for once.

Deuce also murdered a Blood in 2004 and was responsible for at least two other shootings where the victims survived. I had run search warrants with the Weed and Seed team on him seven times–always wearing a black mask. Now, knowing he dealt directly with X-Man, I really wanted him off the streets.

Smurf and I met at Deuce's supply house, where Smurf worked, selling around a half-kilo of crack cocaine per day for Deuce. Deuce had already made his morning drop and wouldn't return until the next day. We hung out and set a plan into motion as the customers came in and out for hours. Yes, sir, Tee from the Westside, kin in the Fishbowl, was about to move his game to Poly but winning wouldn't be easy. In a sense, this felt like starting over again. The most significant difference was that I was positive that I could pull it off. The progress in the Bowl showed me just how effective I'd become. My confidence would show to these newbies in Poly, too.

My research panned out on this deal as well. As it turns out, Deuce was Tre's cousin and a proud member of the infamous Douglas crime family. This was an awesome connection, but I tempered my excitement, as I knew there were "cousins" all over the hood who never even communicated. Smurf didn't know Tre, so that was my frame of mind going forward – but I'd certainly keep it in the back of my mind to use when necessary. Nothing beats a bad guy vouching for me to another bad guy – especially when they are real family, extended or otherwise. Smurf had known Deuce for 11 years and had been working for him the last couple of months. I figured between Deuce's trust in Smurf and my connection with Tre, I'd get close to Deuce sooner or later. As it turned out, it would be later.

Like his predecessors, X-Man and Nasty (X-Man's right-hand man), Deuce was coming up fast. He was a Crip through and through and was very proud of his affiliation. His love for the gang he belonged to would ultimately contribute to his demise. He was so dedicated that, even under incriminating police interrogation, he wouldn't deny or downplay his role as a gang leader. The most disturbing example of his eternal allegiance came when I learned he had named his son "F.D. Hoova," which was short for the "Five Duece Hoova Crip" gang set he belonged to. That was the type of absolute social ignorance I had to work with. These guys plowed through life with nothing to lose. Deuce was a violent, sociopathic killer. He played his gangster role like an A-list actor, creating enemies all over the city. He treated his women, his workers, and his gang foes all the same – like trash. The difference was that although he routinely assaulted his women and workers for minor violations of his fragile ego, he never killed them. He redeemed those passes to hell by only off-ing his sworn gang enemies.

I started spending quite a bit of OTB time with Smurf, hanging out at Deuce's supply house. I became familiar with the daily operations and hoped that by being there so often, Deuce would relax enough to deal with me. Deuce started tasking Smurf with holding anywhere from a quarter to three birds for him at the house until he needed to cook or sell them elsewhere. This was a bad situation for Smurf and me because there was perfectly good dope for the taking, and neither of us could do it without getting burned – or so I first thought.

Smurf called me one day and said Deuce went to Houston for a couple of days and left two birds at the house. A single bird for a guy like me at that time ran about $16,000. The exposure and length of time it would remain there made me crazy. I brainstormed for any way I could get my hands on that dope. Only Smurf and Deuce knew it was there, so if it came up missing, Smurf would surely die. Suddenly, a light bulb appeared above me. I tilted my head slightly and rotated toward the camera and smiled with revelation. Often in these types of instances, I had my most creative ideas. Other times I tended to overthink and turn what should have been a simple plan into a cluster. This light bulb had the cluster in it all the way, but sometimes, I cannot see past the lightbulb itself.

I decided to buzz a rookie narc we lovingly called "The Count." He was a short, funny, Hispanic dude with a mustache and goatee that made him look like The Count from Sesame Street. He was inexperienced but anxious to work, and this assignment would be right up his alley. I snagged a spare ride from the narc office fleet, gathered a team of narcs and patrolmen at a nearby police station, and briefed my idea. Smurf would wait in the house near the dope. Next to Deuce's house were two wooded lots. The two birds were stowed under a log in the woods near the house. So, I staged a fake car chase. I assigned The Count to drive an unmarked car about a mile away from the target, who would then refuse to stop for an approaching patrol unit running lights and sirens and attracting attention and neighborhood onlookers as they went. The Count would keep driving at the posted speed limit to avoid an actual accident that would certainly screw me until he reached the wooded area next to Deuce's. At that point, he would bail out and run from the pursuing officers, who also would stop and abandon their vehicles to pursue the terrible Count on foot into the woods. Once they all disappeared into the woods and out of sightline from the road and gawking neighbors, additional patrol units and a K-9 would be called in to help search for the fleeing Muppet. By then, half the neighborhood would be out witnessing the brilliant, entertaining events unfold. While hunting The Count in the woods, the K-9 dog would "hit" on the birds. When The Count got caught, we'd put him and the dope on display for the onlookers. When Smurf had to explain the outlandish story behind the missing dope to Deuce, he'd have 20 neighbors corroborate his tale. Genius? If everything went without a hitch, maybe. But how often does that happen?

My buddy Scott "PAB" McCarthy from Narcotics and I set up down the street from the target and hid in an unmarked van to watch the genius plan unfold through binos. I took a deep breath as I looked over at Scott and nodded. With a smirk, I radioed the "go" signal.

Within minutes, we began to hear sirens. As they got closer and closer, I felt like I was watching a movie as my heart raced in anticipation of The Count's big screen debut. People were already starting to gather outside to see what was going on. It was working. Suddenly, about a quarter of a mile away, I saw plumes of dirt. Only seconds later, the Count's car slid around the corner on two wheels, spitting rocks that had settled in the street crevasses and pushing at least 60 mph in the residential zone! One! One mistake, ah, ah, ah! So much for following the plan. In disbelief, my heart dropped as I watched my plan further unravel through plumes of dirt, loud motors, and sirens, times three. We started laughing hysterically. What else could we do? Lord knows I'd need a sense of humor for the next snafu, too.

When The Count reached the lot in front of the woods, he tried to stop, but he was going too fast. He oversteered and slammed the brakes, causing his car to hop the curb and careen straight into a light pole! Two! Two mistakes, ah, ah, ah! The police car stopped safely behind him. There was a slight pause in the action. I'm quite sure this was the point where The Count began to wonder if he was still going to have a job when this was finished. By now we were laughing so hard, I was crying and actually had to concentrate to hold my bladder. My laughter replaced what should have been shrieks of horror. Finally, The Count's door opened. The settling dust from the street was now replaced by smoke billowing from his hood. But then, a short, squatty, purple Muppet donning his famous black cape emerged from the smoke to save the day. It was…The Count! He immediately and laboriously launched into his 25-second 50-yard "dash" into the woods. The neighbors, now out in full force, witnessed this police catastrophe. The patrolman had to wait several seconds before pursuing to make sure they didn't inadvertently overtake the speeding purple streak before he reached the woods.

My phone rang. As I attempted to answer it, I was laughing so hard that the person on the other end hung up, thinking he must have had the wrong number. When he called back, I realized it was Smurf.

"What's up, bro? Are you in there watching this?" I asked, still giggling.

"Yo, Tee, man, is all them police because of you?"

"Well, yeah, you know it's that time."

"Hey, well, yeah, I tried to call you Tee, man. I just got out the car with Deuce."

I was silenced with a moment of anticipated terror.

"We just picked up the birds and took them to his other house. I tried to call you man! Tee! Tee? You there?"

I hung up on him as my partner looked at me quizzically.

"Sometimes my guy is a little air-headed," I told him, "But this is ridiculous." He knew the plan, and then Deuce showed up early and quite unexpectedly wanted to get the birds. So instead of calling me, he goes brain-dead, leaves with Deuce and the two birds, yet does nothing about it until the Muppet Show completes its curtain call! This cluster just got clustered, if that's even possible."

The Count was eventually caught and arrested. To the novice onlooker, it was a textbook arrest of a dangerous Muppet fleeing from police after crashing his car. In reality, not one thing went right. I watched in disbelief as officers handled a large crowd, six police cars, one wrecked unmarked police car, two K-9 dogs, and one purple Muppet with no dope. I had some explaining to do.

As it turned out, Deuce had gone down to Houston to attend a party for a popular rapper. He acted like "Mr. Kingpin" and made it rain in front of a bunch of wannabe players, blowing through $15,000 in a day and a half. Needless to say, he had to come back early to get some of his dope moving, recoup his losses, and ruin my day.

Things eventually cooled on my end following the Count fiasco. As time passed, so did my anger at Smurf. He resumed working for Deuce, although I use the term "working" for Deuce very loosely. Deuce was basically robbing Smurf. Guys like him relied on intimidation to overcome his poor working relationships. Smurf made only pennies on the dollar for the large amounts of work and risks he took doing it, which began to take a toll on his ability to stay afloat financially. I was throwing some money at Smurf for helping me since, by this time, his case was dismissed for info that led to other busts I gave my team. But with my limited budget, I couldn't help much. Something had to give.

My phone rang. I was asleep for once. It was Smurf. It was close to 1 a.m., so I figured it had to be important.

"What you need, bro?" I asked in a "sleep voice."

"Tee, you gotta help me, man, he said; he's gonna be back in an hour, and he's gonna kill me if I don't got it by then!"

"Whoa, whoa, whoa! Calm down and start over."

The story unfolded and went like this: Smurf was into Deuce for a measly $200, and it was way past due. So, Deuce and Tre stopped by the house to confront him about it – yes, Tre! Deuce asked where his money was. Smurf said he didn't have it, but he would get it to him soon. Then Tre stepped in and told Deuce:

"Man, you gonna let him punk you like that? He ain't respectin' you when he takes yo money? Beat his ass, or you the punk!"

Smurf was sitting on a small chair playing a video game, staring at Deuce as he began to stew. It didn't take much to convince a violent bastard like Deuce to go off, and Smurf knew it. He tried again to explain he'd have the money soon, but before he could, Deuce grabbed a two-by-four from the corner we'd used as a doorjamb and started whaling on Smurf. Smurf raised his arms to protect himself, to no avail. When Deuce finished, he gave Smurf the ultimatum:

"I'm comin' back in an hour. If you don't have the money, I'll kill you."

"And that's when I called you, Tee. I gotta get that money, man. He's serious!"

I had no choice. I knew what Deuce was capable of. I snagged an icepack from my freezer, jumped in the Benz, drove to my bank, withdrew $200 of my own money, and then headed out to the hood. I called on a brother officer I knew was working the area that night and told him where I would be. He agreed to stand by and monitor me on the cell phone.

By the time I got to Smurf, it was at least 1:45 a.m. I gave him an icepack I'd brought from the house. He was already swelling up like crazy and had gashes and scrapes on top of that.

"You ready, Bro? We don't have much time. Hold this on your head, and let's go get this done."

"I'm ready. We gonna have to go to his family's house though to give it to him."   Great, I thought. I'll be OTB with minimal cover, and now I'll be going into an unfamiliar house with a pissed-off Deuce. At least I'd bolster my cover while I was there. And truthfully, I was pissed. This was ridiculous after all the work Smurf did for this POS. Either way, $200 was a drop in the bucket for Tee from the Westside, who was about to make another debut at a big-timer's casa.

We got to Deuce's house by 2 a.m. I noticed an extra vehicle in the driveway, but I couldn't make out what it was. The house was located along a relatively busy street, but as was the norm for these spots, the lighting was horrible. The house was surrounded by several trees, a large porch, a burglar-bar door, and a locked perimeter fence – typical. I pulled up, parked unobtrusively across the street and about 25 feet back from his front door. With no real plan and knowing full well what could happen, I called and connected phones with my guy. Smurf and I hopped the chain-link fence, went up the porch steps, and he knocked. Deuce slung the door open immediately and eyed Smurf.

"This better be good," Deuce said. I could tell he was still pissed, but he ignored me.

"I got you, bro," Smurf told him submissively. "Cash money."

"C'mon in, but he stays," Deuce said as he pointed to me. Smurf looked at me, and I waved him on.

"Go ahead, dude, I'll just hang here." We were in no position to make demands with no true cover.

From the doorway, I spotted Deuce's wife and son. But then my heart raced a three-second-flat zero-to-60. I spotted X-Man! He was standing at the living room table near an SKS assault rifle laid out within reach of anyone in the room, including the kid. I handed Smurf the money as he went inside to show Deuce I was the man. I prayed this would all be over without a hitch. It was way too early in the morning for more problems. As Smurf went inside, I held my breath and listened intently. It was miraculous I'd made it to this point. I was both excited and worried at the same time. I tried to stay composed as I waited the grueling 120 seconds before Smurf finally came out. He was alive – and smiling.

"Tee, you ain't never gonna believe who's in there!"

"I saw, bro. X-Man, right?"

"Not only that, him and Deuce are cookin' product in the kitchen right now!" Smurf exclaimed. "They got guns all over the place, too."

"Just get in the friggin' car, man. I'm just glad you are in one piece."

We drove to a secluded lot and started jotting details of what Smurf saw on a napkin. That's how I always took notes. While undercover, I always needed to be able to jot down ideas, plate numbers, names, and addresses but still be prepared for unexpected passengers. With the napkin notes, if a bad guy got into the car, I'd wad the notes up and shove them in the side of my door like a snot rag. No one would want to mess with that. On the other hand, I would be screwed if the bad guy were to get in and find my dumb ass with an organized sticky notepad and a Police Officer's Association pen. So, nap notes were my thing.

Then Smurf said, "I got you something else, too, Tee."

I was afraid to ask.

"Deuce said to give you this."

Smurf handed me a small baggie of coke. It was a sample of his latest and a gesture of thanks for covering the debt. I later told my boss (mostly) about what happened, and that the urgency of the situation caused me to use my own money. He reimbursed the dough, and I tagged the powder as evidence without disclosing locations or suspects as was my way. And once again, because of my great supervisor, I dodged a procedural bullet.

Deuce had let my foot in the door whether he knew it or not. But I still had a lot of work to do, and despite careful planning, Tee's next leap forward into the Polywood Crip world would again come by accident.

CHAPTER 10
"Bad Boys, Bad Boys, What am I Gonna Do?!"

I was making slow-but-sure headway with Deuce, but I needed to actively look for new sources so I could attract Crips to work with or for me in the meantime. To compound the issue, Smurf seemed to be getting depressed. He substantially slowed the flow of info I had been getting from him; most days, it was difficult even to find him.

I was concerned for him, so I decided to leverage a strategic move. In August 2005, I called up an old informant from my Weed and Seed days, "Redd." Without disclosing the fact that Smurf worked for me or what project I was working on, I told Redd to make a buy and stir up a little convo with Smurf at Deuce's supply house. I needed to see what was wrong with Smurf and get some new leads. Maybe a new face would get him talking because he sure wasn't talking to me.

Just like the old days, I gave Redd some score money and watched from a cleverly hidden spot as he walked up to the house. A new guy they called "DP" opened the door. Redd asked for Smurf, but DP said he was out. Well, so far, his luck matched mine. I watched carefully as Redd went into the house with him. After about 10 seconds, they came out together and walked around the corner to a spot on Hanger Street. This house sat high up on a hill, a perfect vantage for running a dope operation. The lookouts could probably see for blocks from the front windows. Redd and DP went into the Hanger house, and after about a minute, Redd came out alone and met with me.

"No Smurf?" I asked.

"Nah, he wasn't there, but the guy who was there, DP, said when they out of dope, he takes everybody to the dude around the corner to score. I guess he's supposed to be connected to Deuce in some way. Look like he bangin' too, by the looks of his tatts."

"Polywood?" I asked.

"5x2 Polywood, straight up", Redd said. And Redd knew his stuff.

This was news to me. Although I knew about the house on Hanger, I had no idea until now that there was any connection to the guys in my case. Of course, I had never been to Deuce's when there wasn't dope to be sold, either.

The very next day, I spent several worrisome hours combing the hood, cruising the blocks with a 40-ounce in the front seat, and hunting for Smurf. I had to see what was wrong with that fool, who had no adult influence. I hit all the usual spots we'd go. I hit the car wash on Rosedale, the convenience store on Vaughn where we often met and bought our rollin' 40s, his ex-girl's house, Deuce's spot, and even his mama's work. He was really starting to worry me. Finally, in the most ironic place of all, Hanger Street, I spotted the bastard from behind, walkin' away and about a hundred yards in front of me. I gunned the Benz. As I got close, I yanked the e-brake, tapped the foot brake and turned the wheel sharply. My tires screeched spectacularly as I executed a textbook J-turn. I slid past him, smoking the tires, and came to a stop, now facing him. He'd heard the screeching and, thinking he was about to be run over, literally jumped 2 feet in the air and off the curb. As the rubber-laden smoke blew clear, he stood up and wiped the dirt from his knees.

"You just gonna ignore a brother forever?" I asked matter-of-factly.

"Tee, what the fuck! I think I shit my pants!"

"You deserve that, you elusive son of a bitch," I half-joked. "Now get in. I'll get you to a restroom to change, but then we gotta talk some real talk."

We chatted for over an hour. I broke down every reason why it was important for us to keep in touch. Professionally, he knew the rules and he'd obviously broken them. But if there was something else bothering him, even something personal, I was ready to hear that, too. I explained that this wasn't a do-or-die gig for him anymore. His participation was voluntary, and I recognized the insane risk he was taking on. We both were taking on great risk. The main issue was that if we were working as a team, we must communicate – or the other could die. It was that simple.

"Tee, I feel you. I've just been having some issues with my girl and shit's gone sideways a few times, that's it. I'm fine. I didn't know you really gave a shit like that. I mean, we's workin' out here, but I just thought…

"I got you, bro," I said. From now on, we got each other's backs – on the real tip – not just to knock down some target. Feel me?"

We shook on it. Our talk brought us into a new stage of our relationship, and fast. It had to happen, though. Trust out here is tough to come by and silence makes your imagination go wild.

I eventually told him what I'd heard about the spot on Hanger Street. Smurf knew exactly what and whom I was talking about. I was perplexed as to why he hadn't given me this info before. But I discovered the answer as soon as he told me his baby brother ran business for the guy there. The guy, "Yolo," was a Polywood Crip connected to big dope.

"Let's get to know ol' Yolo, and I'll keep your brother out of the mix. But you have to promise me you'll start meetin' me every day so I can make sure you're cool. You disappear, and I start to wonder about you. I'll keep green in your pocket, DP out of the loop, and you keep your head in the game. Deal?"

"I can do that for ya, Tee," Smurf said, smiling. I could tell he was excited that I'd so easily let his brother off the hook and about doing something new. Hell, I didn't care if I had to let one measly slinger go by while I reeled in dozens of others – especially knowing his brother would be getting him out of the game altogether. It was the end goal that truly mattered – downing X-Man and his whole op to salvage innocents.

We drove back to Yolo's that afternoon. It was a scorching hot day, much like the entire summer had been, but for some reason, today seemed worse. It was 102 degrees, and my pants were sticking to my legs like meat in Saran Wrap. During this investigation, I wore long, baggy clothes and usually a cap of some kind. I wished we could meet Yolo in the shallow end of a community pool somewhere, but this would have to do.

I had high hopes as Smurf and I walked up and knocked on the Hanger house door. DP answered and let us right in as soon as he saw Smurf. They hugged and Smurf introduced DP as his brother, even though his brother had no idea who I really was. This was the same brother who inspired Smurf to switch sides in the first place. I'd definitely keep DP off paper for Smurf's sake – and to keep my word.

I met three other hustlers inside. They were all young Crips with seemingly no significance. The house was stripped with only the bare necessities: a couch, a TV with video games, dope, and guns. And although I couldn't see it in the open, I was certain there was a Bible and porn in there somewhere. We always joked amongst ourselves in the Weed and Seed Unit about determining whether a house was a true dope spot or not by busting down the door and finding a Bible and then porn of sorts. Once we did, we knew the dope was near, and we kept looking.

Yolo was due to drop the supply any minute, so we all hung out and waited for him. We talked about my background and business deals as they smoked weed and blasted some decent hip-hop. As usual, I sat in a strange living room with strange people I knew to be dangerous and guns lying out in the open. It was beginning to feel normal to me, and that was not good. When there are guns inside a locked house full of gangbangers, there should be what I call controlled fear. Controlled fear is a good thing. It's the fear you feel before going on stage, before a public speaking engagement, before parachuting out of an airplane. In law enforcement, it's the fear that causes you to remain careful in a dangerous situation. Training and experience will determine the amount of fear you can control so you are never paralyzed by it, but there should always be some fear. I was experienced in recognizing and functioning within high-risk and undercover situations and hand-to-hand combat, so I should have been more concerned with my environment. But this time, although I'd instinctively positioned myself to kill and escape, I was also consciously worried by the lack of fear I felt.

After a while, Yolo pulled into the driveway and came inside. Unlike Tre or Deuce, he was unassuming. He had a thick build but was only about 5'9", with only the essential tatts. DP and Smurf made my intro. Yolo was cautious, as most were the first time. Outside of a weed distribution charge, he had a fairly clean record. Being cautious probably kept him out of jail, but I didn't trust him, either. My instincts told me this guy was trouble, and I learned to always trust my instincts in this line of work.

We discussed a little business, and Yolo suggested we do a sample deal through Smurf the first time, and then we'd see how things went. That sounded familiar. This guy knew what he was doing. I gladly agreed and waited outside as Smurf scored the sample. Now I had another name to drop, but I wasn't obligated to Yolo because he was still playing scared. Over the next few days, I went to the Hanger house several times alone – sometimes to hang out and sometimes to do business. Before I knew it, I scored from Yolo a few times a week. I was getting really good at this.

One day, I stopped by and found no one at the house. As I hopped into the Benz to leave, a dude I'd met there before signaled to me from down the street and came up to my window.

"Say, Tee, can you get me a bump on the powder real quick?" he asked. "I can pay you in a few hours."

"Listen bro, you know someone like me can't be carryin' that stuff around all the time, or the heat around here would take it all. Besides, how do I know you would pay me?"

"You see that house right up the street there?" He pointed to an old, but well-kept house, three doors from Yolo's. It was the only house on the street with fresh flowers in the beds and a wooden "Welcome Home" sign, nostalgically posted by the door.

"Yeah, that's the old lady's house. What about it?" I knew it well enough since I'd been hanging around lately.

"I'm fixin' to kick that door. She gots a decent TV and my homeboy already gots a buyer for $40."

I'm trying to stay cool. "Man, you oughta leave her outta that kid shit and hit some of those bangin' fools around the block who keep shootin' at us. Thing is, I ain't got nothin' for you right now anyway, but I could tell DP to hook you up."

"Shit, she ain't home, I know. Probably ain't watchin' that thing anyway. I'll catch up to ya later, Tee."

I watched in horror as he walked straight for the poor old lady's house to burgle her TV and kicked her door in. No class at all. I split and called my buddy working patrol and explained the deal. I told him to get out here fast because this idiot was taking the TV and leaving. My friend was puzzled.

"If you saw him do it, why didn't you stop him?"

No one would understand why I didn't stop the burglary at the time it happened. They had no idea how deep my cover was on the street or how huge this case had become. Not even my boss really knew. Like I said, I only shared info that absolutely had to be shared. The less people knew, the less chance there was that I'd be burned. This deep an operation was and is so rare anymore, especially on the local law enforcement level. There was no way I was outing myself now. I was finally getting to the big fish.

"Brother, do you trust me?"

"Yeah," he answered suspiciously.

"Then please don't ask me why. Just know that if I could have stopped it, I would have. Now get over there, dude!"

My friend arrived too late to catch the burglar. I called the detective in charge of the case and loosely explained my situation. I identified the kid. Per my request, the detective sat on the case for a while to avoid burning me but put the fool in jail for the burglary. I tried to buy the TV back from his homeboy, but he had already resold it and didn't know where it was. After all was said and done, I decided to buy a new TV for the poor old lady myself. I delivered it anonymously. I made sure she was home, then I put it on her front doorstep, rang the doorbell, and split. It would take her old self a good minute or two to get up and answer the door. From up the street, I watched her retrieve it and the note I put on the box that read: Have a nice day! I felt a little better about the whole situation, although I'm sure she'd soon appreciate getting the gangbangin' jerks off her block even more.

As it turned out, I'd have several interesting experiences while seeking an absent Yolo at his Hanger Street spot. Another day, as I left Hanger after missing Yolo, I ran into Smurf, who had just come from our convenience store at the end of the block. Smurf hopped into the Benz to chat when a homeboy of his he called Noochie pulled up next to us in his gold Lexus.

"Whassup, Smurf? You guys lookin' to score?"

Smurf looked at me for the answer. I discreetly displayed a Crip hand sign and shrugged, as if to make sure this dude was claiming. Smurf nodded.

"Yeah, man, this my homeboy Tee. He's helpin' me come up a little, but Yolo ain't home."

"Yeah, I seen you around here man. Nice ride. I can hook you up, whatcha need?"

Turns out Noochie was small-time, but in my experience, some of my best connections came from small-timers. Small-time hustlers are, by default, the hardest workers and are more easily motivated by money. We agreed to follow Noochie to his house and check his work. Maybe I could make another connection in X-Man's op.

Back when I was in patrol, I managed to star in a couple of TV episodes of COPS. Why? Our supervisor assigned officers who hustled and got into stuff when the film crew arrived. So, I didn't volunteer, but it still turned out to be an interesting experience. I still get a few calls from friends all over the country who catch a rerun and realize for the first time that I was on the show. It was important to remember that most jails in the mid-late 90s only carried local TV channels. Because the old shows run so often on local TV, the bad guys become regular viewers. I have had more than my share of unnerving conversations while undercover about their interest in it.

Smurf and I pulled into the driveway behind Noochie's Lexus and followed him into the house. It was a shotgun house that looked like it had to be at least 50 years old. A window A/C unit ran full blast to keep the temperature below 90 inside. It smelled like an old sock (not my favorite). It wasn't unkempt, but it certainly wasn't comfortable either.

As I looked around, I saw carefully separated piles of crack cocaine on the living room table beside a box of Baggies and a scale. As I continued through the room, allowing my senses to guide me through the house, I suddenly froze in fear. I recognized the voices on the television. What were the odds? I turned slowly toward the TV, grimacing as if I were about to be hit, and then I was. Oh, how could I have been so stupid? "Officer Tegan Broadwater" was displayed on the screen – plain as day – running his mouth – on COPS – in full uniform – and arresting some poor dope dealer, of all things! Then I snapped out of it. I had to act fast, or I was dead!

The guys were mingling near the coffee table, so I immediately positioned myself in front of the TV. The TV was set against the west wall, and the couch was set against the east wall, with only the living room table and me separating them. Unfortunately for me, with Noochie's dope on the living room table, he planted himself on the couch facing the tube. Smurf's dumb ass went over and stood right by Noochie, which didn't help me a bit. He was supposed to be helping me! I wasn't at my very best because this was likely the most unpredictable thing I could have encountered. I interrupted the conversation and proceeded to filibuster, determined to keep anyone from recognizing the voices behind me. As I spoke about God knows what, I kept trying to raise my voice above the one on the TV that just wouldn't shut up. Noochie had to think I was crazy, but I was determined to avoid certain doom.

Finally, my eight-minute episode ended after what seemed like the time equivalent of Alex Haley's Roots in slow motion. I then hastily looked to finish the deal with Noochie and say goodbye. I couldn't leave fast enough.

"Shit! I appreciate this, Noochie, but we gotta get this done and split. I just remembered, I gotta be downtown to meet my parole officer in 10 minutes, so I gotta buzz!"

"You got it. I be down there this Friday."

We swapped green for white, and I bolted. In the back of my mind, I still feared that Noochie would realize what was happening and that I would be tailed. I hurriedly got in the Benz. By the time Smurf got in, I was already backing out of the driveway. Pulling off, I checked my six and launched a heat run. I wasn't being followed.

"What the hell's up, Tee? Why you in such a hurry?"

I looked at Smurf. He was sitting there with a truly puzzled look on his face.

"You really don't know, do ya?" I asked.

"No. What?"

I paused for a second and then thought better of answering. The last thing I need is for the two of us to be worried about that kind of thing happening again.

"Nothin' Smurf, it's nothin.' I do have to get somewhere, that's all. You did nice work, bro."

I dropped Smurf off. He had no clue what was going on. He didn't even think I acted weird at Noochie's. I must have been on autopilot. I wiped the sweat from my brow and exhaled. Man, I wish I hadn't done that friggin' COPS thing!"

Weeks passed, and I was still doing a lot of business with Yolo. My case on him was firm and I needed to find a creative way to move on. I decided to tell him he was too unavailable, which was actually true. He wasn't even at the house much anymore and was slow to deliver my orders.

The next day, as I drove near the Hanger Street house, Smurf waved me down from our convenience store lot. I pulled over and he hopped inside.

"What's up, Tee?"

"Nada bro, you know anything good?" I asked.

"Yeah man, you know Lil' Saint?"

I looked at Smurf with a snide grin. "Do I know Lil' Saint? Do I ever! I've been kickin' in his doors for years!" I exclaimed. "He back out?"

"You want him?" Smurf asked.

"Where to?" I asked as I whipped the Benz around the parking lot to head out.

Lil' Saint was a punk. He stood all 5-foot-8, constantly battled with his weight, and had a smooth, girly face that would make any Hood Princess jealous. Lil' Saint had great connections, though. He claimed to be a gangbanger, and the Polywood Crips accepted him as one of their own, but he really didn't fit the profile. He talked the talk but apparently never walked the walk. Outside of slingin' tons of dope, being tight with the bad boys and carrying guns he would never use, he was harmless. Up to this point, I had arrested him a dozen times on my search warrants. But when I ran search warrants, I always wore a mask to hide my identity, and that's not exactly personal.

Because I had run so many warrants on him, I had a real good idea his business was always booming, having talked to the arrestees snitching on each warrant. I had targeted a handful of important people in this operation who I could reach by leveraging Saint. I was surprised he was back out of jail and was anxious to hook him.

Saint wasn't there when Smurf and I got to his house. I sat in front of the house for a bit just in case he showed up, but he never did. But in a stroke of more bad luck, Yolo did drive by and see me in front of Saint's house. Apparently, I was being disrespectful by sitting at a different dealer's spot. At the time, I thought nothing of it and just waved as he passed, but I would soon face yet another cluster.

When my phone started ringing super early the next morning, I was not awake yet, so I ignored it. If it's important, they'll leave a message. Besides, my phone rang all day, every day, because of this job. The phone rang again and again and again. This is a sign an informant is calling. They know that with me, you have to blow my phone up 800 times in a row to convince me there is an emergency. That's because it's not usually an emergency but a plea for money. No such luck this time.

I finally answered. It was Smurf.

"Tee, man, you gotta get out here; there's a problem with Yolo."

"Aw geez, what now?" I asked reluctantly.

"He put a jacket on you, man! He's tellin' everybody! He even told Saint and DP!"

I was perplexed. A "jacket" given to someone means they are labeled a snitch. When you try to give somebody a jacket on the street, you'd better be damn sure what you're talking about because you are putting a possible death sentence on this person. I was worried about what Yolo knew or had learned. Did he know Big Mask, the dirty cop from the Fishbowl? Did I say something I shouldn't have? Did he watch COPS? I had to find out quickly before this whole operation came crashing down.

I got up and drove into Poly, OTB. Fittingly, I met with Smurf at the store where Deuce and X-Man had done their robbery and murder years prior. We had a long discussion about what could have gone wrong. Smurf was convinced that Yolo's whole problem stemmed from my switching business to Saint so suddenly. It just seemed suspicious to him that I would move from one steady supplier to a competitor on the same level. So suspicious in fact, that he became convinced I was a snitch. If this was true and Yolo hadn't confirmed my identity, I'd need to act fast.

I badly needed Smurf to lobby on my behalf while I devised a plan. I sent him out to talk with all the guys we had dealt with together and tell them that everything was all right and that Yolo was looped to think I was a snitch. Meanwhile, I set up a meeting with Tre. I told him I wanted to discuss some important business concerning one of his homeboys. Tre was the highest-ranking Crip whom I had established a relationship with to this point. Even though he wasn't in Poly, he was still Deuce's cousin and would definitely have some power to control this. He agreed to meet on short notice, and I headed to the Bowl. I decided that much like the way I handled everything else, I would deal with this as if I were hustling dope in real life. My reputation and money depended on the trust of the people I dealt with. I would seek revenge.

I pulled into Tre's driveway around noon the next day, just as he was coming out of the front door. He hopped in the front seat.

"I need to holler at you about one of your homeboys in Poly – Yolo. You know him?" I got straight to the business. And I was pissed.

"I know the fool, but I don't really fuck with him. Why?"

"The bastard's tryin' to give me a jacket and I ain't ready to take that from some punk like him. But I realize if he's your boy, I'd let you know before I did something to him, 'cause I ain't tryin' to get crossways with you."

Tre laughed out loud. "He's givin' you a jacket! Say Tee, you go do what you need to do. You won't have a problem with me. What you gonna do to that fool anyway?"

"I can tell you he aint' gonna like it, but I'll let him live as long as he fixes the situation."

This was going to be a mess. In the back of my mind, I had hoped Tre would handle the situation for me, but that would have jeopardized poor Yolo's life. Now it would be my job to show this moron I wasn't a snitch. Tee was about to cash in a bit of his street cred.

That night, I went home and vented to my wife. This operation was really starting to take a toll on my home life. My personality was changing; I was always stressed out, and she let me know. She didn't know what to tell me when I vented, but it helped a lot to get some of the things off my chest, and she certainly cared – more than anyone else. Of course, the things I told her were a fraction of what I was going through daily, but she didn't need to hear all of it. That would scare her, and she was my life and my rock. I wouldn't wish that upon her.

I didn't sleep much that night, not that I slept much anyway. I knew what needed to happen, but I still tried to devise a creative alternative. I couldn't let Yolo blow my cover and end the operation. I had my solution. There was no other way Tee could handle this. My mind was made up. I turned over to catch a couple of hours of sleep and set my alarm.

My alarm went off at 6:30 a.m. I rolled out of bed and jumped into my clothes. I should have been tired, but I was wired and ready. It was OTB time. Yolo would be at the Hanger house since he collected money there in the mornings. I kissed my beautiful sleeping wife, snuck out quietly, and headed to Hanger Street to handle my business.

I parked the Benz up the street and waited patiently for Yolo to arrive. I think my lack of sleep was calming my nerves. Finally, around 8 a.m., he pulled into the driveway. I was buzzing. Game time. He got out of the car unsuspectingly and headed for the front door of the house. I bailed out of the Benz like a bat outta hell and made a B-line for him. Sprinting up the massive hill, I met him at the porch stairs that led to the front door. He looked at me wide-eyed. I could see the panic in his eyes. It was too late. I hit him with a closed fist one time, square in the face. He stumbled backward as I moved in. I caught him and locked my forearms around his neck, and pulled him down and off-balance, slamming knee-strikes into his ribcage. The first one landed true, as I heard every bit of air leave his lungs. The others would be a gangbanger's bonus. I kept moving in half circles, controlling him by his neck and head as I blasted him with knees, keeping my elbows in and my grip behind his head tight. It wouldn't be worth breaking a hand or infecting my knuckles on this prick after all. Finally, I took a large, circular step back with my right leg and threw him across the yard by his head. He rolled and then slid the rest of the way down the sloped front yard on his back. He whimpered as he slowly came to a stop.

He just lay there for a few seconds as it became eerily quiet. He had the wind knocked out of him, so he couldn't do much else but writhe between gasps. I gathered myself and glanced around for witnesses. It was too early for most out here to be up and around. I walked over to him, leaned down, and whispered in his ear in the best Eastwood impression I could muster.

"Take that jacket off me."

Tee would be doing business in Poly again.

CHAPTER 11
"Oh, When Lil' Saint Comes Marching In"

Yolo split the hood for a while. He moved to a different part of town and got a real job as a delivery boy. That impressed me, since a real job was seldom considered an option for these guys, but it would be a short-lived stint before he'd return to the life. Poly covered a much bigger area than the Bowl. So, when I started making my usual treks through it to stop in, visit bad guys, and keep my face in the game, it was easier to explain that I had some other business nearby when they pushed me to spend some cash. Since Poly turf stretched miles instead of blocks, they'd usually buy the story without being able to check it easily.

On one of those days, I cruised by a spot on Burton Street and spied Lil' Saint's truck in front of the house. I immediately went to Smurf's crash pad of the week and woke him up to ask him if he knew what the scoop was over there. He admitted that he used to sell dope in that house for Saint and a guy named "GG," but it had been quite a while.

"We're payin' 'em a visit, bro. Get your shirt on and let's roll," I told him as I held up a wad of money. "And for heaven's sake, wake up. It's friggin' noon already."

GG was a hardcore 5x2 Polywood Crip with a history of dope and violence, including an attempted murder. Apparently, on a hot summer day a few years back, GG got into it with some rival banger in the projects, and their argument got loud. There was a lot of mad dogging and loud cussing involved. This is typical regarding arguments, but these guys are hypersensitive to disrespect. When you are in a gang like his, it's just as likely someone would be killed over holding up a rival gang sign in your hood as it would anything else.

In this case, it didn't take long for GG to raise the stakes. He finally felt disrespected enough to pull his semi-auto 9mm handgun from the front of his pants and aim it at the guy. A group of girls gathering nearby were trying to converse while this ruckus was going on, and one of them stupidly piped up.

"Say, why don't y'all take it somewhere else! Y'all ain't fixin' to do this in front of my house!"

This was blatant disrespect. GG was handling gang business like a "man" should, and some chick was trying to interrupt him. How dare she? GG turned the gun on the woman and started firing—dozens of people dove under porches, inside other apartments, and under cars. Bullets flew everywhere as GG unloaded.

Fortunately, these guys are poor shots. Unfortunately, if the person they are shooting doesn't die, they get a mere slap on the wrist. Such is life out here in the hood. GG's rounds somehow missed everyone that day. He was eventually caught, arrested and charged with attempted murder. The state ultimately pled him down to an aggravated assault charge, and he was out of jail in no time – only now he had heavy street cred. That was part of the motivation behind Operation Fishbowl in the first place. It was about time for guys like GG to be held accountable.

GG sold coke and got most of his supply from Saint. Saint had his Mexican supplier and was still trying to be Mr. Bad Boy in Poly, but both still answered to X-Man. Therefore, both deserved to go down. Smurf and I pulled into the driveway at the Burton house, got out, and knocked on the door. As the door opened, the guy there introduced himself to me as "Kada," but he also went by "Big Kada" and "Sir Kada Pimp." I'd call him by his first name. Kada had been gangbangin' since he was a young teenager, and he had just recently turned 30. That's old for an active banger but it gave him more time to establish an admirable rap sheet. He'd accrued several dope charges, a couple of assaults, and two attempted murder arrests in his short life. Kada looked mean, too. He stood 6 feet tall, weighed around 200 pounds sans a lick of fat, and was covered in tatts that were easily seen atop his light complexion. His face looked much like Mike Tyson, pre-tattoo. His kind of street cred went a long way in a gang. Although Kada wasn't a big-time dope dealer, he obviously had the respect of his peers.

I introduced myself. He recognized my name, and we were let inside. Kada's girlfriend was chilling out in front of the big-screen TV. Down the hall I saw Saint in the far bedroom with some bopper (female gang groupie). By the look of the growing pile of clothes on the floor, I knew he'd be far too busy to do business with me at this point.

I decided to tell Kada that what I was looking for was a good new source and I heard a guy named GG might be that person. Kada said GG had just left but offered to hook me up with whatever I needed. He assured me his stuff came from GG. I decided to go for it. It'd get me in the door there and maybe Kada would eventually vouch for me. Kada led me into the kitchen, where he dismantled the countertop by lifting the edge of the stove and then prying the unsecured counter upward, exposing a large sack of dope and a digital scale. I still wanted to at least talk to GG, so we did the deal then went back to the living room and hung out. We talked about women and weed but most of the talk was about football. Football season is my favorite time of year and Kada was an NFL fan, too. I razzed him about being a T-shirt fan (liking teams he had no legitimate affiliation with).

"You can't randomly pick teams to follow, man, especially if they're reigning champs. It's against the unwritten rules of fandom," I told him. "Plus, it takes the excitement out of following your team through the good and the bad."

"Yeah, well, the Cowboys suck, though."

"Well said. That's a fantastic argument, dude - until they win. Then you'll be a big fan of theirs, right? Or do you just like teams with cool uniforms?

"Shit."

"The 'Cool Uniform Theory' is only good if you picked the team with the coolest uniform before your 10th birthday, before you knew better. Otherwise, you gotta be a man and stick with your boys."

"Shit man, you crazy dude, the Cowboys suck."

I was cracking up, razzing him, and he was hammerin' back the best he could. This type of banter put my mind at ease with these guys. It's the same way I talk to my buddies in real life. The difference is that I'm talking with a murdering ex-con after a dope deal inside a locked gang house while everyone gets high and bangs chicks behind their wives' backs. My nerdy idea of a good time involved talking smack to my buddies after our kids' ballgame at a restaurant, close enough for now. Eventually, we turned the conversation to business, and I told Kada to call GG for me. At least I had to meet the cat and slide him a little green as a promise for future success. Even my football rants didn't fill the time it was taking for this guy to get back to the house, though. Smurf used my phone to call as Kada gave us GG's digits. This worked out well for me because now I had GG's number in my phone. GG answered, and Smurf talked to him about meeting at another one of his houses on Avenue M, which was still in Poly.

"Let's do it," I told Smurf as he looked at me quizzically, wondering whether to go. It was, perhaps, a little forced, but I was feelin' it.

"Be there in five with my patna," Smurf told GG, and hung up.

I thanked Kada for the hookup, told him to ponder the rules of NFL fandom I'd shared, and we went on our merry way. The Avenue M house was only about eight or nine blocks from the Burton house, so our trip was quick. Pulling the Benz to the curb in front, I realized thugs were everywhere. Smurf went inside to ask GG if he could bring me in and introduce us. GG sent three guys outside to ask me about 832 questions to determine if I was cool. I secretly relish these moments. It's the ultimate test to an undercover officer: the combination of cool improvisation with careful recitation. However, This situation, with Smurf inside and me outside, posed a new set of potential problems. I worried that Smurf might say something contradicting what I might say outside. If he did, we'd be made and not even know it. This could be particularly dangerous around guys like GG, who can freak out and kill without hesitation.

This day, though, I felt I could talk my way through anything. I felt confident and relaxed after spending all that time with Kada. It seemed to take forever, but eventually, Smurf came out of the house unscathed and had a deal done. Although it went through Smurf this time, we made plans with GG to formally introduce and deal for a larger amount later when he was more prepared. I understood. Only a real dealer would have it this way.

The next day, Smurf and I ran into Saint at a local gas station in a stroke of pure luck. He recognized the Benz and me. I teased him about my being at the Burton house when he was with his "date" to remind him I had been dealing with his people and get him to relax. Because I caught him off-guard, I conned him into a hand-to-hand deal on the spot. Saint was now mine. I continued to set my sights on his violent partner, GG. It would mean so much for him to go down. GG was a threat to society and needed to go.

I called GG and set a deal up at a local Poly parking lot. I'd take Smurf since he knew GG and the way he worked. Smurf and I rolled to the meeting spot about 4 p.m. We waited there about 15 minutes before Smurf got on my phone and called GG to see where the hell he was. We put my phone on speaker.

"Say man, where you at?" Smurf asked.

"You there with Tee?"

"Yeah, man, you said the Fina lot at four, right?"

"Say, go to 4-3-1-7 Rufus. My boys'll be there. I been havin' some other shit goin' on for a minute, but I can meet you there in 10."

Smurf hung up. I knew this was another test. I was sure we were being watched to see if we had any police surveilling, which of course we did not – only distant patrol dudes on a cell phone. We headed to Rufus Street. When we arrived, I parked the Benz across and down one house from the target. As we got out and approached the door, I noticed another burglar bar cage surrounding the front door. I knocked, and some fool answered the door. He stared at me like I'd just spit on him.

"What you want?"

"We're meetin' GG," I told him sternly and with a matching expression. I wasn't gonna let this guy think for a minute that he had intimidated me.

He opened the door. Smurf and I stepped inside. As I entered this place, I felt strangely grave as I heard the bar door lock behind me. The front room was a living area with a blanket that hung from the ceiling, covering the entrance to the next room. Around the front room, I saw six people I didn't recognize. They were decked out in typical gang garb and tatts. I noted three guns lying out in the open next to three of the bangers who were sitting in various places about the room. A few were weighing and packaging crack, while the others were hanging out and playing video games. The room was sweltering and dark despite the time of day. I put my back to the front wall nearest the locked door and ran scenarios in my head as to which one of these sorry bastards would die first if I had to make a drastic move.

"You know any of these cats?" I whispered to Smurf.

"I never seen any of these fools before, Tee." By the look on Smurf's face, he was as nervous as I'd ever seen him. "What do we do now?"

"We wait for GG. I'll give him the 10 minutes and then we go, if they let us. Just keep your eyes open," I told him.

This was starting to scream, "set up." These guys could easily have known GG sent me to make a buy and would know I'd have cash. I began to wonder if I could take out all three of the armed suckers before they got to us since they were spread about the room. Smurf was nearly frantic and looking out the window for GG's car. As he did, one of the thugs stared me down and reached in slow motion toward the gun on the living room table. I took two aggressive steps toward him and lifted my shirt, exposing the piece I had on me. He then pulled his hand slowly away and formed a finger-thumb gun with his hand, pointed at me, and lowered his thumb as if to shoot. The whole room erupted in laughter, except for us. Smurf turned back to me.

"GG's here…GG's here…GG's here, man." Each time he said it, his words slowed as he began to breathe again.

GG unlocked the bar door and came in. I introduced myself and joked that his friends were entertaining and that I should invite them to my side of town sometime. GG was pretty quiet and all about business. We agreed on weight and cost. I carefully kept my eyes scanning the room as I counted out my money. GG went to the other side of the room, pulled out a large sack of coke from his pants, and put it on a scale nearby. He bagged what he owed me and held it up. I crossed the room, clinching my wad of $100 bills, still cognizant of everyone around me. I was a sitting duck in that moment, and everybody knew it. I just hoped for the best. I took the dope, paid up and scanned for potential victims.

"Appreciate you, bro," I told GG as we sealed the deal with a handshake.

"Yeah," was all he said. I didn't need to hear more, either. I got my lucky ass out of there.

"Let's roll, Smurf," I said as I stood anxiously by the door while one of the punks unlocked and opened it for us to leave.

"You still gonna come with me to drop that 'green' off to the west side?" I asked Smurf as a front.

"You gonna cut me in this time?" he asked, immediately going with the flow as he finally smiled.

"Just come on, man!" I said and slapped him upside the head. We kept talking crap as we crossed the street and faded to the safety of the Benz. As we shut the doors and pulled away, I asked Smurf one more time if he had recognized even one of those guys.

"Hell no! I thought we was fixin' to get hit by them fools."

"All I know is that it's all good now, and GG's hourglass of freedom just flipped."

CHAPTER 12
"Street Fed"

I pulled up to the curb and rolled down my window. The heat of the summer had finally passed, and I could wear layers of clothes that made it easier to cover most of my body. I also had some hip hats I could finally use. For a Texan, though, this day was friggin' freezing. It was probably only 32 degrees, but the wind was cranked up, and I didn't want to sit there with my window down and talk all day long.

"Hey man, I need to score heavy," I told Reggie as he leaned in the Benz to keep warm.

"I can get you however much you want, Tee. I get stuff from Phat, X-Man, or Nasty. How much you want?"

Obviously, this guy is talkin' out of the wrong end because he's trying way too hard by dropping names like that. This is one way I can tell if I want to bother dealing with someone at all. If he sounds like a cop, he either is one, or he's blowing smoke. Reggie was small-time. He was a cokehead and lived in a house within a cul-de-sac overrun by Polywood Crips trafficking dope. His rent was paid indirectly by Nasty (X-Man's partner) and in exchange, Nasty put his people in place to sell there. To make a buy, the customer had to pull down to the dead end and turn around. Everyone could see who you were ahead of time, and if you were deemed a snitch, you were a sitting duck. It was deadly. There had been several shootings there, but much like the Bowl, it was difficult for law enforcement to nab the people at the top and shut down business.

"Okay, slide me a quick 62 (grams)," I said, knowing full well there was no way he could come up with even that small amount.

"Uh, well, say you can talk to Zule," Reggie stuttered.

"All right, I'll holler at Zule then. If you wanna come with, I'll hook you up with a piece."

Having Reggie with me just looked better. Even if he didn't vouch for me, it was implied. I spotted Zule coming out of the house into the front yard. He was an ominous Crip at 6-foot-3, 240 pounds. He was tatted but lacked the mass amounts of artwork typically associated with these guys. His hair was short, skin bright and he had a very distinctive eye that was albino white. He'd shot and been shot. He'd played the game to the fullest and wasn't done yet. He'd had his chance in life when he got an opportunity to play linebacker at Fresno State, but he came home after less than a full year and got back into the gang and dope game. It was a total shame.

He did make reasonable money taking orders and making deliveries for Nasty, though – around $5000 a month, depending on traffic. Because he was a Crip and ran Nasty's stuff, I knew he always had big weight on hand. He made a great target. Though Nasty paid him well, Zule also sold his own stuff on the side to pad his income even more. That's where I came in. I was trying to come up as far and fast as I could without breaking my bank. Zule was a perfect target for me because he was big-time, being one man removed from Nasty but sold stuff I could still afford on the side. I needed to get him on the hook.

"Say Zule, need a 62," I said as we shook hands, street-style. I was there with Reggie and Zule knew me from being around Poly, so he didn't hesitate to hook me up.

"Come back in 5. It'll be 12 ($1200)."

"My boy will be here in five," I told him. "Hook him up." Who was my boy? You guessed it: Pino.

It was finally time for Pino to start payin' me back. Since he was so huge, I'd just finished using his services (for a small fee and some fun) as my "muscle" on a deal at the Hanger spot a few minutes earlier. The new kid working the house wanted me to float him a little loan for an "investment" and swore he would pay me back in two days. I told him "No" twice before finally agreeing to get him the money he needed. I decided that Tee would benefit from being a player with money if I diversified. I'd pulled up to the curb in front of the Hangar house and handed the kid his investment cash. As I drove away, I had Pino immediately pull up in his own ride to talk to the kid:

"You will come up with Tee's green, or I will personally hunt you down and kill your ass. And pray I don't know where your family is, either." Then he just drove off.

Pino owed me. He didn't know the loan-loaded youngster, so he worried less about being recognized. Plus, it was kind of fun for both of us. This kid was crapping himself. I was brash and confident now. He returned my money a half-day early. He would tell me later, "That big boy of yours is crazy! I would never do you wrong anyway, Tee!" I assured him he was right and the big man would do whatever I told him. It was both adventurous and advantageous to pull off such stunts with these two guys, neither of whom had a clue who I really was. I was establishing myself as a legitimate player in Poly, just as I had done in the Fishbowl.

As requested, Pino pulled into the cul-de-sac and completed my deal with Zule. To keep my word to Reggie, after Pino left, I pulled back down the cul-de-sac and made sure all went well. While I was there, I threw Reggie a C-note and told him to fetch me a yard ($100 worth of crack). He was stoked to make some money off me. Zule was pleased, Pino was pleased, and I was pleased. But as my list of cases grew, so did my need for bigger cash to spend.

I met with my boss, Sgt. Wilson and told him I had hit a crossroads. I gave him a full briefing on my progress and remaining goals. I had so much unfinished business to tend to, but my breadcrumb city budget wouldn't cut it any longer. Wilson had been going to bat for me, covering my butt with the upper brass for my out-of-control spending for months on end. He was ready for me to catch a monetary break, too.

"How about shopping the feds for some support," he suggested. I'd never thought about it but was betwixt. He said he'd make some calls. I was prepared to shop for some federal options.

I wasn't sure which direction I needed to go as far as federal entities went, and I was certainly nervous about exploiting my OTB progress. I had to do something, so I went everywhere. I presented my case as a conspiracy leveraging firearms to promote the sale of illegal narcotics to the ATF (Bureau of Alcohol, Tobacco, and Firearms). Then, I presented to the DEA (Drug Enforcement Administration), highlighting the dope suppliers and trafficking conspiracy links. But I declined to use either of them when I was told they would be interested in taking and working my case without me. F that. I didn't come this far to get booted from my own case. I understood that I'd get very little, if any, credit for my work. That was fine with me. I wasn't motivated by notoriety at all. I wanted this to make a positive difference. Undercover operators rarely get credit anyway; it's just the nature of the gig. But some new entity moving forward on this now huge case without utilizing the only guy who'd been directly involved in the inner workings of the conspiracy from the very beginning seemed plain irresponsible.

My first presentation to the FBI came in November of 2005. I met FBI Special Agent Jennifer Coffindaffer, assigned to the FBI's Violent Crimes Task Force. The unit worked gang cases. The Task Force's goal was to identify, investigate, and disrupt the ever-growing illegal gang and organized crime in the Fort Worth area. Bingo! Agent Coffindaffer was impressed and very interested in the case as I presented it. More importantly, she had no problem allowing me to remain the sole undercover officer in charge. She would offer up her federal case-building expertise through the end of the operation to ensure it was completed, as government cases are often complicated. The only stickler was that she was finishing an unrelated case and wouldn't be able to give me her full attention for a couple of months.

I was ecstatic. I could handle a couple more months alone if I knew I had the right support on its way. After all, of the 41 federal convictions we'd end up with, I'd already sewn up 32 myself by this point.

"One more thing," I told her. "I'm gonna need some decent buy-money for some deals I've worked up next week. I might be better off with some wheels that had advanced surveillance equipment, too. I realize you may not be around for a bit, but I can't afford to slow down." I held my breath.

"How much do you need?" she asked.

"At least $6000 for this week." I held my breath again.

"I'll make some calls and get you taken care of," she told me.

I felt like Tom Selleck, turning toward the camera with a slick smirk and a wink at the end of each episode of Magnum, P.I. I may have been exhausted, but I was immediately reinvigorated by this win. I thanked her for the support and focused onward.

In less than two days I was approved for government overtime pay, was issued a Land Rover complete with secreted audio/video surveillance equipment, and my $6000 cash. Coffindaffer was my new hero, soon to be my new partner, and she was willing to work. Tee was rollin' with authority again.

I was also incredibly grateful that my sergeant believed in the project and me. Very few, if any, supervisors in his position would have gone half this far out of their way to accommodate an old-school, long-term, undercover operation like this. Not to mention, after he'd battled upper management to this point, he would now miss out on the reward of seeing the project through to the end. He had class, though, and he saw the big picture. This wasn't about one person. It was about putting over 50 violent menaces away for a very long time. I had become as close to deep cover as one could get in this modern-day finger-screw, everybody-has-to-know-everything world. Even my coworkers had absolutely no clue what I was doing daily. Some chided me behind my back, while the few others who knew me best also knew that if I was out of the office, I was hustling. So much of my time was spent OTB, no one would really know the enormous amount of time I'd dumped into this except perhaps my most extraordinary wife, Holli. Though she didn't know every detail, she certainly knew enough to notice my growing absence from home. She became my only source of emotional support, and that would save my life. She is the most loving person I've ever known and knows me better than anyone. So, when she voiced concerns, I listened.

Holli supported me but noticed that my outrageous work hours and lack of sleep were beginning to take their toll. I was slowly becoming a different person. Although this FBI involvement was going to boost my case and morale, I was starting to feel trapped in a criminal life I had created and couldn't escape. It was too late to quit and too early to quit. I was taking phone calls and getting out of bed to meet people at three and four in the morning, spending time off the clock, researching and preparing my next moves, and hanging out, playing, working, and drinking with these gangbangers. I seemed to never sleep by this time. I would lie awake and think about the case. It would really make me angry that I couldn't focus on anything else in my life then, yet my anger would fuel the problem and keep me awake longer. I knew there would be an end but couldn't quite see the light. One November evening, Holli finally shone it on me.

We were sitting outside her mom's place after I had to step out from a stress-laden episode I was having in front of her family. The weather was calm, and we just sat in the silence for a moment before she finally spoke her considerate, and conspicuously wise, words.

"You have to do something to help yourself or you are going to have a nervous breakdown," she finally told me. "I cannot help you anymore. I don't know what to do. You've transformed into a different person than the man I married."

Her words pierced my heart. I felt like an 8th-round Foreman in "The Rumble in the Jungle." I sat in momentary reflective silence. How could I continue without my soul mate's support? Answer: I could not. Upon that realization, I knew I had to shake off my concussion and stand. Holli had given me the wake-up call. Not just with her words, I could see in her eyes that she was truly concerned, distraught, and frustrated. She was telling me she was losing her ability to help keep me in tune with our marriage, and that was huge. I couldn't lose her. She is my everything. Her heartfelt words spawned focus and determination for me to live up to my promises as a man. I knew I needed her help, too. Just realizing this allowed me to climb back up the ropes before the ref could count to 10 – unlike poor George Foreman.

Refocused and reloaded, I assured her I would improve all aspects of myself and, in turn, be the husband she knew once again.

In Her Words:
By Holli Broadwater

I never had a problem with Tegan doing his job, but for many reasons, I did worry about him getting shot, or someone following home, or someone investigating him and discovering who he was.

When I would wake up and see he was gone, I would stay awake until he returned. And if I knew he would be out late working, I sat in our living room stressing until he returned safely. The chance that he might not return kept me awake even though I had to work the next morning. During the operation, I learned not to ask too many questions, even though I was curious. He wouldn't lie if I asked him things, so I allowed him to share what he thought was appropriate, so I wouldn't have to hear about the stuff that would just upset me. One day, I remember him coming home after he had obviously been in a fight. I did ask him, of course, but this time he wouldn't tell me. He knew it was best, and honestly, so did I.

I'm so proud of Tegan for believing in himself when everyone thought he was crazy for thinking he could actually get in with these gangs. I didn't think he was crazy at all or even surprised that he got in.

Sometimes, it's not what you are but rather who you are, and Tegan has a heart for everyone. He sees people as people without judgment. He was not the cop who treated people like dirt on the ground. He treated them with kindness and respect. They were from different sides of the law, but that didn't matter to him.

People often ask me what it was like for me, and I always answer the same way: It definitely wasn't the time of my life! But was it worth it? The answer is yes.

He wanted to do this not for himself - or even the police department. He wanted to do it for the families in this neighborhood caught in the middle.

I'm proud of his accomplishments and the courage that he had to make a change to this small east-side neighborhood dubbed the Fishbowl.

Among the many ways I sought help, I prayed and stayed closer to the people who truly mattered to me -- the ones who constantly reminded me of who I really was and gave perspective to a life that only seemed complicated. I'd seen it work before. Back in 2003, I worked a routine case in Poly. I'd made a buy at a house that I thought might lead to bigger and better things. I had a really good narc team at the time. I gathered my team, and we went over my plan to hit the house with hopes of finding some dope and flipping a dealer or two for their sources.

We stacked in the raid van and checked all our equipment: raid vests secured, weapons locked and loaded, bolt cutters, pry-bar and battering ram on hand, helmets and masks ready, and of course, the slammin' music in the CD player.

This op was no different. We pulled out of the secret narcotics office location and headed to the target with Rage Against the Machine cranked to 10. We slung a few jokes back and forth to keep it fun, and then we neared the target. The van grew silent as about half of us dove into some prayer and prepared to bail out.

When we pulled to the front of the house, we had to stop in the middle of the street; the drug traffic was so bad. As we bailed out of the van, people scattered like roaches. The perimeter team was tasked with catching the runners outside the target. We stayed focused and speed-walked to the door. The biggest guy on the team moved to the front of our line and swung the 50-pound ram like a 12-ounce tennis racquet, blasting the door off the hinges with one hit. We stormed in shouting orders: "Police! Get down!" I was first through the door. We entered and quickly broke into teams of two, hitting each room and taking bad guys to the ground as we passed through. As I reached the rear of the house, I saw a large dark figure dash across a hallway. It was Deuce. I gave chase and hollered commands to get down as my teammate, Kyletto, joined me. After a mild struggle, we caught up and politely slammed him to the ground. He wanted to fight and was still reacting to our surprise attack, but then, realizing quickly how stupid it was to resist, he complied.

In all, eight bad guys were detained in a matter of 20 seconds by our team of seven, plus two officers manning the perimeter. It was a routine execution but was deemed merely a mild success when we discovered only traces of the dope we had hoped to find. I had all the detainees separated and interviewed. By doing this, I learned they distributed from this location but stored the big stuff in a house across the street. Now they tell me! These guys were not stupid; they constantly posed challenges like this to guys like me, but I love a challenge. There I stood with friggin' Deuce, face down on the ground, and nothing to charge him with. With my face covered in a narc-standard balaclava, I actually congratulated him but told him this wasn't over. This became part of my inspiration to go deep undercover. It did seem like a tricky proposition, but it would allow me to get the types of intel, like the storage house across the street, for myself. Incredibly, though, Deuce would become the least important part of that day. My life was about to change again.

One of the people who did end up arrested that day was a multi-racial, single mother, gang bopper, and only slightly discreet dope trafficker named Nikki. Nikki was outside the house that day getting ready to deliver a dope order into the house but was caught by the perimeter team before she'd even made it out of her car. The case I had on her was open-and-shut. There would be no problem getting a conviction. Her criminal record was so extensive I could hardly believe she was free. She'd also admitted that the stuff we caught her with was hers, so I believed she was toast.

Something strange happened, though. She told my boss she wanted to speak to me. I sat and talked with her when I finally had a free minute, mask-to-face. People who are busted will often say anything to keep from going to jail. If these same people go to jail, they reach moments of clarity, get saved, and swear that if we could get them released, they'd never return to crime again. Statistics speak volumes about how these narcissistic, sociopathic, manipulating users rarely do the right thing in these cases. Despite this fact, I try my best to remain objective and listen.

It felt different as Nikki began to talk. She seemed truly sorry and sincere when she spoke of wanting to change for her children's sake. As I normally did, I told her she'd have to start giving up information on the dealers she knew, but I wanted her to think about that first. She and I both knew how dangerous those people were, and she also needed to consider her kids. I told her she would still have to go to jail and to call me in three days. Usually, by that time, the feeling of sudden inspiration and desperation has faded, and most won't even call, let alone stay repentant. Not Nikki.

She called me after she bailed out of jail on the third day.

Over the next several months, we'd visit. We eventually bonded and developed trust. So much so that I removed the mask and began working to help rebuild her life. The intel I leveraged from her was just that – intel. I didn't want her putting herself in harm's way making buys. Nikki had been a small-time dope runner for big Polywood CRIP suppliers for as long as she could remember, and this would be her only ticket out. She would need a lot of help from me, though, because she had been in so much trouble in the past. I approached Judge Wayne Salvant and Chief Prosecutor David Hagerman in Tarrant County, who was assigned to her case and in charge of revoking her probation. Fortunately, they were both very compassionate people. It took a long-winded speech and a personal promise that I'd be personally responsible for Nikki to convince them to grant her probation and not lock her up. Now, my reputation was on the line.

Nikki provided key player insights as was required by the judge. After that, I focused on getting her away from the influences keeping her and her family down all these years. Her only "friends" to that point were all dopers and bangers. When she quit working for them, they all quit being "friends." She soon moved to a better neighborhood, got and kept a job, learned how to write checks and pay bills, and resumed raising her children to the best of her ability. As more time passed, I even introduced Nikki to Holli. No one in this world is as caring or generous as my wife, which solidified the relationship between our families. We often hung out, provided birthday parties for the kids, and generally tried to contribute to her family's happiness whenever possible. Nikki and her kids became an inspiration for me and countless others who saw what could become of an abused, drug-addicted, parentless, uneducated single mom with kids. To me, it illustrated the fact that my daily struggles paled in comparison to so many others. It was pure perspective. To this day, our families are close, and we continue to watch Nikki personify the poster child for success.

This experience also presented a deeper Polywood perspective for me. Though I still worked and hoped for more expeditious progress into this Crip conspiracy, I could never have anticipated the sudden appearance of one ultra-foe that would deepen the plot.

CHAPTER 13
"King of the Blocc (Party)"

To fend off my nervous breakdown and preserve the man I knew I was, my wife, my son, and I started spending a little more time with Nikki and her kids. As I rejuvenated, Smurf did as well. Perhaps he had also felt my attitude slump. We met up one December morning, and he said he had a good lead for me.

"Tee, I got us a meet with Kendrick.

"Say, you know if I can connect the dots, I'm in. He still claimin' [a gang]?"

"Of course. And he said he seen you in Poly. I told him you runnin' big game, and we should hook up."

Kendrick was a Crip supplier who had been eluding me for some time in Poly. He brought kilos of dope to a house near the Bideker dead-end that was converted into crack by some Crip cooks there. I'd seen him at this house a couple of times while I was there buying. Kendrick would come back after his stuff was cooked and deliver it to his customers all over the place. He didn't run a dope house. He just took phone orders and met his customers in their vehicles wherever he designated.

Smurf and I drove to a hoppin' barbershop about a mile from the Fishbowl. I pulled in, Smurf hopped out, and went inside. When he returned, he told me Kendrick agreed to meet me up the street at the corner store. I saw Kendrick walk out of the barbershop and get into his Suburban. We followed him to the store. When we pulled into the parking lot, he motioned us to get in the Suburban. I still had no mobile technology from the FBI at this point. I'd periodically use my cell phone (when I wasn't using it to connect to cover) to record some of my conversations with these guys. Although I was not too fond of the idea of using a recorder on a first date, I decided I'd record my meeting with Kendrick. I was trying to bring this gig into the modern age despite my disdain for most of the unreliable tech of the time. I was running this whole operation in an old-school fashion, after all, but I figured I could always learn a little. I got in the back seat and Smurf got in front with Kendrick. It was the most tactically sound place for me to be.

"Whassup, man, I'm Tee. Good to meet ya," I said as I leaned up and shook with Kendrick.

"Hey, bro. Kendrick. You the Tee I seen on Bideker before. You scared me to death the first time I saw you."

"Me? Shoot! Walk in my shoes a minute. It's like friggin' Sesame Street; guess which one doesn't belong. You ain't the one that needs to be worryin' man, trust me!"

He started laughing. We talked for at least 10 minutes. When it came to discussing business, I threw out the fact that I'd been working with Tre, but he was starting to flake, and I needed a more reliable source. I figured he'd know Tre, but not particularly well since Kendrick dealt mostly in Poly. Kendrick had stuff with him, so I convinced him to sell me a yard for my customers to scope. It may have taken me 10 minutes of schmoozing to get him to sling, but it only took one second to be thrown into jeopardy again. Just when I thought things were going perfectly, my phone recorder started beeping.

The primitive P.O.S. had run out of time. It had never done that before, so it caught me by complete surprise. Kendrick and Smurf turned from the front seat and stared at the phone. We were all freaked.

"What the hell's that?" Kendrick asked suspiciously and with a hint of anger.

I know I was blushing because I could feel the heat from the blood rush through my face. This totally sucked, but it didn't stop me from flowing, though.

"Aw, man, this phone is a friggin' piece! Must be tellin' me it's about to die again. I can't keep the battery up for more than a few hours before it dies. I should get it on a charger. We're straight anyway, right?" I asked him to divert focus. Then, there was a distinctly silent moment. It was probably only 3 or 4 seconds of silence, but it seemed like a full minute under the circumstances. Finally, Kendrick piped up. "We straight, Tee. Good meetin' you, dude," he said, completing the deal and convinced of my story. Then we all got out of the 'Burban. Smurf had to grab some cigarettes and scammed me for some cash to get them. When Smurf ran into the store, Kendrick quickly pulled me aside.

"Say Tee, you way too big for that fool, Smurf. You need to quit messin' with him. I can hook you up factory direct."

"Say, I wouldn't mind getting' some reliable work for a change," I told him. "If that's you, then we'll see."

"Remember my digits. Stick 'em in your dyin' phone and call me tomorrow," he told me.

As he rattled off his digits, I kept thinking, "Wow, this is getting easier," as I memorized his number and promised to call.

I thanked Smurf for the hookup. He was as high maintenance as a person could be without demanding exclusive designer accessories, but he did good work and was learning how to do it better every day.

The next day, I called Kendrick as soon as the Crime Lab notified me of the positive dope analysis.

"Kendrick, its Tee."

"What up, Tee? How'd I do?"

"Did good, bro. Need to come holler at ya."

I met him later that day and just shot the breeze, mixing in a little business. Over a few weeks, we ended up with four solid deals on the books. The last deal I did was the most significant, though.

I met him in Poly after ordering some coke in late December. It was nearly Christmas, and I was in good spirits. So was Kendrick. I picked him up, and we rode around the hood. We'd stop off and cut it up with the local bangers hangin' on the corners and yards. It was a great opportunity for me to shut my mouth and listen intently as these fools expatiated on their criminal accomplishments. Kendrick had knocked down a few drinks and talked a mile a minute. I liked Kendrick. He was personable and certainly, one of the easiest guys to talk to. After blowing himself up as the big man and dumping all kinds of gratuitous personal info on me, we did business.

"This is the best, Tee. I only got the best fa ya," Kendrick said as he set a load of crack on the scale I kept in the Benz.

"Yo, wait! Ken, I thought I told you I needed the soft! I can move some of this no sweat, but I really need the powder, like now. You got the reach to hook me up or what?"

"Aw Tee, man, I thought you meant you wanted all hard this time. I cook 95% of my stuff. I wish I'd known earlier because I just got this stuff slammed (cooked)."

By forcing Ken to change my order on the fly, I'd hoped to get to his supplier. Since I knew he was out of the powder, he'd have to hit up his source to make right by me. We had known each other well enough by this time that I figured he would not hesitate to show me his source, either. And he didn't.

Within minutes Kendrick was on the phone calling another infamous Polywood Crip. When I heard the name, I secretly celebrated. This guy was a neighborhood staple and on my list of targets from the beginning. He went by Beelo on the street. I shouldn't have been surprised to hear the name because they'd done business before. I'd just never seen it. Beelo was a bona fide 5x2 Polywood Crip, but he didn't have a rep for being one of the particularly violent ones. Everybody knew and respected him. He was a big-time supplier, a mild-mannered businessman, but spent much of his waking life high on that Ganja.

Kendrick had me drive to Beelo's house in Poly. Beelo wasn't there yet, but Ken said he'd be there "soon." It was an old-fashioned block party at ol' Beelo's joint, though. Ken and I hung out for a full two hours, talking to everyone who came up to make buys and bangers who stopped over to gamble or smoke. I wouldn't usually wait this long for an order of dope, but this was different. We were there to hang out as much as we were to get my order done. Besides, I had told Kendrick I needed the stuff by that day, so I made the time to hang out.

While we chilled, Kendrick talked about his big house, his big money, his big game, you name it. But then he segued into a rant on his big family. Again, my perspective and moral philosophy were challenged by his supposed adoration for his wife and kids, yet he chose to do this "job" and put them all at risk. I was disappointed, amazed, and angry at the same time. I was determined to unlock the secret that would help guys like Kendrick make better decisions and contribute to improving our already-jacked-up world, not making it worse. But that was for another time. All I could do now was focus on my journey at hand.

It was common for bangers to pull up and hang in and around their cars. Some were inside the house, too, but we stayed outside, where the party was expansive. It was amazing that I'd not known about this place before. Dudes were pulling over their cars and cranking tunes while others walked through yards and visited through car windows with homies. It was an impressive impromptu jam.

Soon, it got dark, and it became harder to tell who people were when they pulled up. I saw and spoke to several of my suspects in this case from different times, including Terence, Saint, and Zule. These were all guys I had a rapport with, so the conversations were good, and the pressure was low. And just when I thought things couldn't get any better, they did – for once. A blue SUV crept up, paring the crowd that spilled into the narrow street. Everyone, including Kendrick, saw that ride trundling into view and immediately reported to the street to greet it. I followed, curious and excited. As we reached the majestic SUV, the tinted glass on the rear passenger window slowly lowered. Within seconds, the descending glass revealed the prize behind door number one. It was the king: X-Man himself.

There must have been five or six other bangers in the truck with him, but I was fixated on him. He talked with everyone outside from his hood chariot's rear seat. I decided to move closer to see what I could stir. I stuck close to Ken to blend with the group surrounding their leader. X-Man was a rock star in the hood. The way these guys flocked and verbally sparred for the floor was fascinating. It brought me back to the day I met Gotti. He was a tyrant yet adored. This was the same feel. I kept my eyes on X-Man. Finally, he looked my way.

"Whassup" I said inaudibly, as I tipped my head.

"Whassup," he nodded, keeping his conversation with his adoring fans flowing. He'd periodically look in my direction, though I could only feel him looking because I'd made a point to involve myself in other conversations and not stare any longer. He saw me in the proper context, so I was cool with that.

Just then, Kendrick asked if I was ready. We walked over to the Benz and hopped in with X-Man looking on. That had to look cool, too.

"Drive to the Wreck Shop, and we'll get Beelo there," Kendrick told me.

The Poly Wreck Shop was a meeting place for only the top dog Crips. It was so exclusive that not even my informants could get inside the place. There weren't many actual deals going on there unless they were insiders. They also had a mini recording studio inside. This was where talented rapper "Twisted Black" often hung out, spit lyrics, and smoked with the bangers who occupied the rest of its space. But Black had recently caught a case sellin' work across state lines and was now behind bars. That was such a shame. The dude was makin' some real headway in the music industry and could have put his city on the map. Twisted Black was an extremely talented storyteller. He'd talk about street life, his surviving a gunshot to the face and slingin' dope but say it in a captivating way. So, I would miss the opportunity to meet Twisted Black, but I still had work to do.

I pulled into the lot between two late 80s model Caddys, and Kendrick made a call. Beelo came out of the Wreck Shop, and Kendrick got out of my car to meet him. After a few seconds, they both got into the Benz: Ken in the front and Beelo in the back. We made proper introductions, then I drove them back to Beelo's house.

When we got there, we hung out and talked while Beelo finished his joint. Then I told him what I needed and how much. He got out of the car and went into the house for a few minutes. When he returned, he sold me the brick of coke I'd waited so long to get. It may have taken me five hours from beginning to end, but within that time, I'd accomplished what could otherwise have taken weeks.

Ken had become my latest unwitting informant. Like Ced, Dank, and many others before him, he vouched for me to new players around the hood. Things were going well. Kendrick had so many connections, and I was eager to expose them. My paperwork had increased remarkably since being assigned to the FBI, so I barely kept up with the fast pace and great strokes of luck. But my luck would soon run out as quickly as it came.

CHAPTER 14
"Calling in Sicc"

By January 2006, I had been undercover full-time with Operation Fishbowl for over ten months. Things had worked out very well, but I was exhausted. FBI Agent Coffindaffer finally closed out her other case and would be giving this operation her full attention. I welcomed the help. One of the first tasks we took together was identifying Kendrick's other big connections and ultimately going in for X-Man. Besides Beelo, Ken was pretty sensitive when talking to me about his suppliers. He liked making money off me and knew that if he gave up his sources, I'd move on to work with them, much like he encouraged me to abandon Smurf when I met him. I understand that's how it is, but it made my job much harder.

I was starting to give up on the idea that Ken would ever give up any of his other sources, so Coffindaffer and I reviewed some alternatives. She suggested, as was the typical way the feds worked these types of cases that we try putting a tracker on Kendrick's infamous Suburban. It would be an FBI-installed, hard-wired tracker that would typically take up to 25 minutes to install properly, so we'd have to devise a legal ruse. I hated it. The idea of bringing other law enforcement people into play with one of my guys just turned me off. Though she was experienced in the federal way of doing things, and I wanted to trust her as she did me.

Coffindaffer handled the paperwork, got the tracker approved through the FBI offices, and contacted an on-call tech squad to be ready. I rounded up five reliable narcs and had them meet us in a public library parking lot near one of Ken's drop-off spots to brief them. The plan was to find, tail, and collect intel on the places Kendrick went to for as long as it seemed practical. Then we'd have some marked police units pull him over, hoping to arrest him for dope in the truck or possibly some traffic violation. If we couldn't arrest him, we'd have to find a legal reason to at least detain him away from the truck for as long as it took the tech squad to install the tracking device. My old-school ass wasn't used to dealing with this kind of technology, but I began to accept the idea because it was an outside-the-box tactic – my favorite.

After I briefed the team, they headed out to find Kendrick. Within minutes, they were on him. They tailed him as he made stops at ten different locations for short periods. They copied addresses and plate numbers and wrote descriptions of the people he met. We knew there must have been deals going down, but we wanted as much information as we could gather before making a move. Hours passed as we continued to tail him.

Finally, one of my narc brethren phoned me and said his supervisor wanted the Suburban stopped now. At the time, I hadn't realized his supervisor was even involved. It was such bullsh that the Narc Unit ran things so haphazardly. It fielded all these complaints, and supervisors and certain unmotivated officers alike would become impatient and demand an arrest be made so they could check the stat box and move to the next complaint. It frustrated me and did nothing but perpetuate the dope problems with no real solution in place. And now that I was working on a long-term solution, they wanted to screw it up.

The tech squad hadn't arrived from Dallas yet, so I told him to ask the supervisor if we could hold off until they arrived. Just then, I heard officers on the radio calling out to dispatch that they were stopping a blue Suburban for a traffic violation. We were screwed. The tech team was still 25 minutes out. We barely had a legal stop and, therefore, hardly had a reason to hold him long enough to get the tracking device installed, even if the tech squad were here.

Coffindaffer immediately got on the phone and put a rush on the squad as I pulled across the freeway from the traffic stop to observe and advise from afar. My fellow narcs handled this cluster of situations the best they could as I held my breath. Kendrick was the only occupant in the Suburban, as we already knew. I watched from a vantage point about 200 yards away as the narcs moved him away from the truck and to the rear of the police cars. The darkness and flashing police lights would keep Kendrick from seeing anything in the direction of his ride.

The tech team rushed and made it to the scene in 20, which still seemed like an hour to all the officers stalling on the scene. Meanwhile, said officers were carefully and methodically searching Kendrick's Suburban inch-by-inch after he'd given them verbal permission to do so. Fortunately for us, his truck was an utter mess. It took officers a long time to go through all the clutter inside, which would buy us a little time. I had the tech team pull their vehicles in front of Ken's truck and as far away from him as possible. I sat helplessly across the freeway and watched. There were two police cars with flashing overhead lights behind the Suburban, with Kendrick now inside the second one. There was also a police car in front of the Suburban with lights flashing. At least nine or ten street cops and narcs were standing around watching. The techs slid underneath the Suburban and began their "covert" installation.

It was certainly hard to imagine Kendrick would see anything but officers and flashing lights from where he was sitting. Unfortunately, it would be hard for anyone else to see, either. This is when the second wave of bad luck rolled in. No sooner had the techs crawled underneath the Suburban than a random car pulled over about 100 yards behind the traffic stop. I radioed that a car was up the road so officers could deal with it in case it was a threat. Then, as quickly as it had arrived, it pulled right back onto the freeway and disappeared. Thirty seconds later, while the techs were still under the truck installing, they heard a female voice.

"What are y'all doing under there?"

"Uh, looking for illegal drugs?" one tech guy answered off-guard. He wasn't exactly trained to improvise.

Just then, a uniformed officer noticed the female had breached the nine-man perimeter and asked her name. It was Kendrick's wife! Some ally of Kendrick's must have seen the Suburban stopped and called her. She'd been dropped off in the cover of darkness by the car that had stopped so briefly and walked up to the installers. We were busted. The guys played it off the best they could, but she wasn't buying it, and neither would Ken. The tech team quickly grabbed their equipment and split. No dope was ever found, and Ken was released on the scene. Coffindaffer and I looked at each other in amazement. This was not supposed to be so difficult. But this was also why I hated using all this technological crap. It was a rough start to a new partnership, but I hoped things would improve. No such luck.

I made a few more calls to Kendrick after that incident, but he was too rattled by the stop to do any more business. We talked about everyday life stuff, but every time I brought up business, he would distance himself. He knew he was being watched, and although he likely didn't know where the heat was coming from, he was playing it safe.

"Tee, I told you I'm gettin' out this game, man - quittin' completely. I got my family to worry about. But hey, you and me is some good friends now, so if you wanna go fishin' together or somethin' give me a call, okay? It ain't gotta always be about business anyways, bro."

Dang, was he trying to make me feel guilty or what? Actually, I did feel bad until a close and trusted buddy of mine, Garrett Hull, who worked on a Fort Worth narc team, called and told me he had been spotting Kendrick making his usual delivery rounds again. I should have known it was all bull. I'd scared him off. He was a dope dealer pretending to be a family man, not the other way around. I saw this in many other bad guys who whine about missing their families when they get caught and face the prospect of not seeing them again. But if they're not caught, they only think about themselves as they sling dope, gamble, shoot each other, father illegitimate children, and play gangster and robber. I said goodbye to my guilt but re-swore I'd try to contribute to better solutions to this issue.

I was at another crossroads. Over the next couple of months, I worked with Agent Coffindaffer on some deals Smurf set up with Poly targets. I also tied up a few more deals with some Crips in Poly and the Bowl on my own. Meanwhile, Kendrick was my last real lead into the upper-echelon players. I'd already finished making cases and moved on from so many others that I wasn't sure I had anywhere to go.

I talked to Smurf about it, and we came up with an idea. He had recently spoken with a guy close to the Bowl, an up-and-coming dealer. He was a Crip and most recently was working under Deuce. His name was "Sicc." He ran a couple of houses and an apartment "home base," where he did much of his cutting, cooking, and weighing. Smurf and I had already been to one of his houses several times, but I'd never considered the house or Sicc a target until Deuce's name was brought into it.

I called one of my trusted friends to cover me when we pulled into Sicc's apartment complex for the first time. Smurf went in the first couple of times and tried to get Sicc to come deal with me outside, but instead, he'd send workers out to deal with me. Finally, one day he did come out after I suppose I'd passed his test, and we did biz by the Benz. He was cautious, but I was going to up the ante.

Coffindaffer had hooked me up with proper money, so I planned to use it. One day, I was hanging out in Sicc's apartment complex, buying from a guy named Jay who worked for Sicc.

"Say, ask Sicc if he is big enough to go large. I got some paper (money) burnin' a hole right now."

"Like how much?" Jay asked.

"Let's start with say, a quarter-bird hard, then we can jump up from there if things work out. Think he can handle that sample?"

"I'll talk to him. Call up here in a couple hours."

I called Smurf and asked him to go hang out in the complex while I left and waited for Jay. As I started to pull out of the apartment complex, I was flagged down by a wannabe gangster decked in Crip garb. He came up to my window and introduced himself.

"Say, dog, Nado. What's up?"

"All right. Tee." I introduced myself with a shake.

"Just saw you talkin' to Jay. You need something cuz I can hook you up."

"You don't even know me fool, and I don't know you," I said.

"Man, I seen you up here a bunch of times, man. You dealin' wit' Sicc or who?"

"I'm covered, bro. I appreciate it, though. I'm lookin' for bigger stuff than you are probably used to, anyway." I told him that, sure that he would leave. He just looked like a small-timer.

"Just give me a shot man. Let me roll wit'cha and I'll show you my spots where I can get you whatever."

This guy was really pushing me. I figured he was either one of Sicc's guys testing me, a hustler who wanted a few bucks on a deal, or he was going to rob me.

"Get in."

Nado and I talked business for over 30 minutes. We stopped by three or four spots he was supposedly involved with, and he introduced me to his crew. He asked how big I could go and where I was moving my work. I told him nobody but a cop would ask me that. He laughed and said he was afraid that's what I was.

Now, I was concerned. This guy comes to me and won't leave me alone until I roll with him to scope his spots and meet his homeboys. He is pushing on as if I'm the big boss. Yet he now says he suspects I may be a cop? I'm thinking robbery about now. I was still stuck in my car, too. This is the worst place to be attacked from unless you can pull off in a hurry – which I wouldn't be able to do with this jackass in my passenger seat. I ran scenarios in my head and positioned my piece to give me the best chance to kill the bastard if he tried anything. I decided to try changing his mind with some verbal b.s.

"Say, I know you wanna do business, but I hope you ain't lookin' to close no deal right this minute cuz I gotta go collect some cash," I told him.

"I'm not messin' wit' you, Tee. I can hook you up."

"That's great, I'm just sayin', dude. You may have to chill for a minute." I paused. Then popped the question that could call him out and even the playing field. "You strapped?" I asked.

"Yeah, you?" His honest answer surprised me.

"Yeah."

I flashed my piece. It's a scuffed five-shot revolver, easily hidden for undercover use. I had it tucked in a leather holster half-eaten by my dog about three years before. It didn't look like a gun a cop would be carrying. I wanted him to know that I'd waste him if he had any ideas about robbery. Just then, he pulled out a .9 mm Taurus from his Dickies and showed it to me. We were now on a level. I felt better at least knowing the score. He even let me hold it and check it out. I dropped the magazine and checked to ensure there wasn't a round in the chamber. There wasn't. I'd kill him faster than he could think about robbing me anyway, although I was starting to think he might just be plain crazy.

I eventually admitted to him that I was planning to score a quarter-bird of crack from Sicc.

"I can get that for you in no time, Tee. My homeboys slammed a whole bird at the apartment this mornin'."

"You with Sicc or what?" I asked him suspiciously.

"Well, kind of. We work together a lot, but I got my own hustle goin' on, too."

"So, if I scope your work, it's really gonna be Sicc's?"

"Same exact," he told me. "But way cheaper, fool. Like I say, I'll hook you up. But I am gonna have to see that green first, you know what I'm sayin'?"

I had another genius idea, only this one didn't involve electronics or Muppets.

"I'll tell you what. You give me the mag outta your .9 mil, keep your head down while we cruise to my casa, and I'll snag cash there. I can't let you see where my spot is, but you can see the cash. Then I'll toss you your ammo when we get back to the apartment. You know what I'm sayin'?"

I was beginning to feel like I was in a friggin' movie, but I was flipping the script and taking control. I was intimately familiar with a 5,000-square-foot, $1.9M vacant house I'd use as my base. It was perfectly nested in a neighborhood where I used to work off-duty jobs. Since I'd worked there, Holli and I would frequent it to jog or take my son trick-or-treating. We'd toured this home for sale, pretending to be serious buyers. I'm not sure if the real estate agent was buying our act, but house hunting was a hobby Holli and I dug, even when not in the market to buy. Either way, this would be a calculated gamble that could take me to the top or convince him to rob me for sure. Either way, I was prepared.

He agreed to the deal. I took the magazine out of his pistol and patted him down for any other hidden weapons. I was in the Benz that day, so he put his head between his knees and stared at the Mercedes logo on my floor mat as I headed to my mansion to collect a few thousand bucks. I already had the cash on me, but I didn't want him to know that. About 20 minutes later, I pulled into the driveway of my mansion and told him he could look up.

"I'll be back in a sec, bro," I told him as I hopped out of the Benz, "unlocked" the gate, and walked around the house toward the back door. Nado sat there with a look of pure disbelief and said nothing. I returned and got into the car after hiding around the rear of the house for a couple of minutes. I didn't even have a key after all, but I knew I could open the front gate and walk around back as if I lived there.

"Dude, you live here?"

"Enough with the questions, bro, let's do some business." I flashed my wad of cash at him. He grinned. "Now get that head back down so we can get outta here."

I drove Nado back to the apartments and saw Smurf outside hanging. He came over to the car and talked with Nado and me. I told Nado I trusted Smurf and that he'd have to witness our deal. Smurf got in the backseat. I counted out the cash in front of Nado.

"Don't you try to screw me, Nado. There'll be more where this came from if you're straight," I told him. "But if you ain't..." I looked at him angrily, all the while thinking of Yolo and hoping this would be different.

"I'm straight, Tee, I'm so straight. I can have it ready in an hour or so. I'll call you."

As Nado got out of the car, I re-pocketed my cash and discreetly handed him the magazine to his .9mm and my phone number on a napkin. Smurf and I talked for a few minutes, and I explained what was going on. He agreed to stick around and watch Nado and Sicc prepare my work to ensure it was all good. I told him to call me when it was ready and let me know if something looked crooked.

About 45 minutes later, Smurf called and said it was ready. I told him to meet me in the parking lot in front of Sicc's apartment. I called on an ex-partner of mine, John-John, whom I had trusted with my life many times before, to cover me from across the street. When I pulled in, it was pitch dark. The apartment complex lights were out, and we were in the back where even the moonlight couldn't see. Smurf got in the back seat, and Nado got in the front. I looked back at Smurf as if to ask him to keep his eyes on Nado while I recounted the cash. When I'd finished, Nado pulled a huge sack of crack from the front of his jacket and put it on my scale I'd set on the center console. I turned on my interior light for a split second and then back off. I didn't want anyone to see us there with a wad of cash and dope, but I needed to get at least a quick look at the crack and read the scale. I didn't really have much reason to doubt anyway, since I'd managed to insert Smurf inside as Nado and Sicc prepared the stuff for me.

The scale looked good. The weight was a bit under, but not enough to gripe about. I grabbed the sack of crack and handed it back to Smurf.

"Double-check that, bro. How's it look?" I asked.

"It's straight, Tee. We good," Smurf said confidently as he handed it back to me.

I gave Nado the cash.

"Holler, bro," I told him as he tucked the cash away and got out.

"I'll be here, Tee."

I talked to Smurf for a few minutes and noting all the details of the cook from his end, and then I left him there to hang out some more. I called John-John and told him the deal was good and thanked him for having my back, as usual. Then I made a heat run, dropped the dope into evidence downtown and requested a rush on the Crime Lab analysis. I went home a happy dude.

Late the next day, I got a call from the Crime Lab. As they spoke, the camera rapidly zoomed in all the way from 20 feet to my astounded face. I wasn't prepared for this.

"We are so sorry, Officer Broadwater, but your evidence tested out negative," the tech said, perhaps equally amazed. "We even tested it 3 times to make sure. It certainly looked real."

The dope from Nado was no good! I couldn't believe it. Desperate to establish this new connect, I'd let myself get too anxious. I dropped the ball. Smurf had dropped the ball. Nado certainly had balls but was about to lose them. To think I'd come all this way, made hundreds of buys in this operation, and I get burned now? Yolo thought he had a problem when he crossed me. I'd be lucky to keep my job when I finished this son of a bitch off.

I called Smurf and gave him a lashing.

"How could you not know the stuff was bunk? You were watching them, right?"

"Tee, I swear it looked tight! I had no idea, man!"

The stuff certainly did look good; I could vouch for that. The fact is I should have checked it with a field test kit. I was just too concerned with flipping on lights and getting Nado out of my car so I could deem this thing a success and not get robbed. I lived and learned, but I'd also have a lot of explaining to do.

I hunted Nado over the next couple of days. Day and night, I searched - OTB and otherwise. He had purchased a cheap car with my cash and was hiding out in different places. I'd decided I was going to beat him senseless – in front of all his peeps. The timing was essential. There had to be witnesses. The message needed to be broadcast in the most impactful way possible. Not just a few licks like Yolo, either. This bastard would visit the nearest hospital. I knew I could get in trouble, but I had a cover to maintain and if I let this happen without severe consequences, the next guy would be liable to try and rob and kill me both. Also, simply arresting him would blow my cover instantly, and when all the guys I've dealt with discovered who I really was, I would be hunted down.

What happened next was either an act of God helping me keep my job or another cog in the house of bad luck I had been building; I wasn't sure which. I discovered Nado had been arrested and was being sent back to prison to serve out a three-year sentence on a parole revocation. He'd been pulled over and busted with some dope. I had mixed emotions when I heard, but at least I was still employed. I had to believe that it was an act of God saving my butt when my common sense was lost. It would certainly be par for this course. I wondered if this was the sign I'd reached an end. I would be devastated to finish without a solid case on X-Man. I had been working Fishbowl for more than a year straight now, but I didn't have the sense of satisfaction I needed. It was as if I had made a birthday cake and left off the candles. I wanted candles. Then I wanted to blow them the hell away and get my wish: X-Man.

But X-Man, feeling the heat, had bolted from Fort Worth for a while. The word was he had gone to LA to spend time with his O.G.'s (original gangsters) in Compton.

Over the next few months leading up to May 2006, Coffindaffer and I finished tying up a few loose ends linking my Crips in the Fishbowl conspiracy together. I was almost done, whether I wanted to be or not. However, there'd be one last stand, and it would come courtesy of Deuce, my favorite gangsta.

One of the spots Nado took me to meet his crew before he ripped me

My $1.8M undercover residence

Tre's old block after the roundup and redirection of the neighborhood

Fishbowl Layout (Copyright Google Earth)

Tee and The Rover

Accepting one of the unexpected awards for the operation
(L to R: Assistant U.S. Attorney Mike Worley, me, FBI Special Agent
Jennifer Coffindaffer, U.S. Attorney Richard Roper)

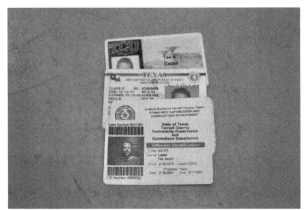

Tee's I.D.'s

Holli and Tee - post Fishbowl

COPs

I thought this episode would never end!

CHAPTER 15
"A Trey, From Downtown"

FORT WORTH — One man was arrested Thursday, and police were searching for a second suspect in connection with the fatal drive-by shooting of a 20-year-old man Wednesday night.
The man was shot once in the buttocks as he and others gathered outside a relative's home in the 1700 block of Colvin Street. He refused to tell responding officers who were responsible, saying only that he knew who did it and would take care of it himself; homicide Sgt. J.D. Thornton said.

He was pronounced dead at John Peter Smith Hospital at 8:22 p.m. — two hours after the shooting — from internal injuries of the abdomen and chest.

Thornton said a gang officer recognized the description of the white four-door car used in the shooting as that belonging to a 27-year-old known gang member. Officers went to the gang member's home and detained him, he said. He was arrested early Thursday on a murder warrant at the downtown police headquarters after investigators identified him as the man who had been driving the car from which the shots were fired, Thornton said. Thornton said investigators have also obtained a warrant for a second man who witnesses have identified as the shooter. That man had not been arrested as of Thursday afternoon.

Thornton said the shooting appears gang-related and may have stemmed from previous altercations among the victim, the suspects, and their relatives. He said the altercations included other shootings in the past weeks.

A young Crip from the Bowl named KiKi got into an argument with a Crip from another side of town and one of Stick's robbing buddies named Ray. KiKi eventually split and went back to the Bowl. Later that same evening, Ray returned to the Bowl determined to avenge what he thought was disrespect. He drove by and shot KiKi as he stood outside the west entrance's lookout house. Phat was there when the police arrived and tried to start a riot against them for clearing the mobs away from KiKi as he lay dying in the yard. Phat was arrested for disturbing the peace and showing his ass. KiKi passed away hours later. This event signaled that my undercover work in Operation Fishbowl was winding down and reminded me that we had to lock these guys up…and soon.

I called a meeting with Smurf in April of 2006. Of the nearly fourteen months I'd been working undercover inside Operation Fishbowl, Smurf had been riding with me for eight. Bug had bolted to south Texas when the feds became involved. He'd heard too many horror stories about informants getting screwed by the government. I didn't blame him, either. He'd done plenty. Things were beginning to wrap up, and cases were solidified and tied together. But this meeting wasn't about tying loose ends or solidifying squat. I told Smurf in no uncertain terms that we had one chance, and only one chance, to make a final run at X-Man. Word had gotten around that X-Man would be making his heralded return during a party in the park for all Crips, 4x3 and 5x2. All would come together on this day. He'd made his announcement, and all were ready.

So what do a bunch of cold-blooded killers and drug dealers do when they want to hold a big party? They obtain a city permit, of course. As strange as it seemed, sometimes the Crips acted like a bunch of Rotarians that could succeed in a world of legitimate business.

The "Four-Tre/King X-Man's Return" party was to be held the weekend following the Crips' self-proclaimed "4x3 Day," which is, logically, April the third of every year. It was purposefully delayed to accommodate X-Man's arrival, but it was very organized. It would also be a grand opportunity for Smurf and me to get some work done. I figured X-Man had been out for a while, so he'd need to create a buzz for his renewed big business. At least, that's what I'd hoped.

The big day rolled around, and I got with Smurf early. People were already starting to hang out near the Bowl, which bordered the park and its party. The weather was perfect. The smell of flaming barbeques filled the air, and loud music blasted from overworked speakers in customized rides. To make myself seen early in the day, I drove the Benz in and out of some nearby apartment complexes, through the Fishbowl and around the park while Smurf hung out with the bangers and put out feelers for any little deals we might be able to work out later.

I garnered some serious looks as I cruised through the park. Everybody was there. Crips from the whole region, which meant even Crips I didn't know, were everywhere. I made the drive through the crowded 10-foot paved driveway a little uncomfortably. There was no way to turn around in a pinch. There was no way to speed away in a pinch. I was getting some high-fives through my window, but more so, suspicious stares and mad dogging. I just had to play this out cool. I wasn't doing anything other than being seen, anyway. Cruising. Establishing myself. I figured my presence would spawn conversations, eventually spreading to those who knew me well, and I'd be vouched for.

This day's idea was one of my oldest: we would spend low and justify the smaller amounts by saying that I'm just scoring for my buddy Smurf so he could flip it and make a few bucks. It was the same MO I used with Bug when this all began, and it had always worked like a charm. I'd use the ruse again since I expected guys to be unprepared for doing substantial business anyway, but I would probably have small stuff on hand since so many people would be hanging out. Ultimately, we needed to find out which dudes we knew would hang close to X-Man. Once we knew that, we'd try and force a deal that would somehow include X-Man in the transaction process – even if his involvement was as simple as being in proximity or, even better, giving the OK for the deal to proceed.

I cruised and did some low-level deals. I hung out with Lil' Saint, Deuce, GG, and a guy named Trace, who also worked with Kendrick. Crip homily spewed by purported do-gooders for the sake of the gang allowed me to listen and learn. But most convos resembled that of typical dudes, too: women, weed, music, and cars. I was beginning to feel like I was back inside my own movie. My tunes were crankin', my attitude positive. Tee was back. But my original optimism was fading. The sun was going down on Four Trey Day, and I still hadn't had my first glimpse of X-Man.

After dark, I decided to search a hood-laden apartment complex across from the Fishbowl. Deuce had been using one of the apartments there as one of his spots for the last few months.

I turned in the main entrance and hooked a left. As I rounded the corner, there it was. The beautiful scene sent adrenaline bolting through my barbequed veins. There in the courtyard, with a crowd of onlooking bangers, playing a game of pick-up basketball, was X-Man.

I hurriedly parked and made my way courtside. I wasn't dressed for the occasion, but I knew an opportunity to jump in the game would afford me some street cred. Yes, I can hoop. I'm not a point-type player, but I am aggressive to a fault. I was certainly as good as this group of street ball wannabees. My video game prowess had served me well with these fools, but this would take the cake!

"I got next," I said, strutting side court next to the waiting reserves.

One of the sweaty losers looked me up and down, then said, "This the final game, playa. Those fools are finnda be 'X-ed' out in the final!"

"Well, damn."

X-Man's team put the last ball in the hole, and it was over just like that. He didn't waste time scootin', either. The second he finished playing, he walked over to Deuce's apartment to clean up and hang out a bit.

X-Man and Deuce were still tight after all these years, even though X-Man was a much bigger player. They strategically teamed to maintain gang strongholds and preserve their history. They were dedicated to the gang life more than almost anyone else I'd seen outside of Phat. Smurf saw the hoops, too, and called me immediately.

"Did you see who was playin' ball just now?" he asked me excitedly.

"Couldn't miss that, bro. Can we get a quick deal with Deuce while X is with him?" I figured maybe since we were already there and they were at the apartment, we could execute the pressure plan, hoping for some ancillary X-Man involvement in it.

"Let me get something, Tee. It's gonna look too small for you. Deuce knows you big-time, and he gone think it's fucked-up if you ask for me since he knows me better."

I checked my ego. Smurf was right. I could try this myself, but since Deuce was around, he'd wonder why I was buying for Smurf when Smurf could go to him directly. As common sense prevailed, I deferred and hoped for the best. This had to work, or we'd be done without an X-Man deal. Hopefully, he'd bite. I prayed.

After a deep breath, I told Smurf, "Get this done. I'll get my wheels and pull around near the front door so they can see us. Meet me there." I figured if I had the Benz, then at least some of the dudes around there who didn't know me would recognize it.

I ran to the car, hauled to the front of the complex, and was lucky enough to find a perfect parking place right in front of Deuce's. As I pulled in, I was instantly surrounded by five gangbangers, two of whom I knew. I thought maybe they were alarmed by the speed at which I flew into the spot.

"What you doin' out here, white boy?" I heard from my passenger side window. I turned to look at the rare fool who hadn't at least heard of me by now.

"Say, Tee! Hey man, he's cool. Tee's kinfolk."

Ahh, the sweet sound of a familiar voice. It was an old Crip-ssociate named Razor. I hadn't worked with Razor in months, but he remembered me well. I'd met him through Ced, my brother from the carwash. Razor was the type that put me through "tests" during the early part of our business relationship. He liked to expose the butt of a pistol in his waistband or pick up an assault rifle in the next room and then mysteriously duck behind a door. All of this inside his house, while I patiently waited. He didn't scare me, but the deals were intense since I didn't know whether he would burst back into the room with my work or the Mac 10. After a few transactions, he learned to trust me, and we were good. Razor was also an aspiring rapper and we'd talked about collaborating on some tracks together. He wanted me to lay some rhythm section tracks and then he'd spit who knows what over it. We became very familiar, but I still didn't trust the guy enough to actually hit a studio, as much as I'd have loved to play. Nevertheless, today I was grateful he was around!

Just then, I saw X-Man and Deuce step out and stand in front of the apartment door to smoke. I had a very small window of opportunity. I looked at Smurf, who was making his way over to me. This show had already started. No time for a rehearsal. As he leaned into my window, I glanced over toward the apartment and then handed him a C-note in front of everybody.

"Tee, thanks as always for hookin' a brother up. I owe you!"

After he thanked me aloud for helping him out, he marched straight up to X-Man and Deuce like it was nothing. He confidently greeted them with his loose, street-style handshake. I couldn't hear what was being said, which made me nuts, and the cats around my car were chatting it up like nothing else was happening. What was worse, Smurf had positioned his dumbass right in my line of sight while he chatted the kingpins up. But as good luck would have it, they shuffled around and even walked slightly toward me. They finally wrapped up their convo and stood, by chance, just in front of my car. Now I had the perfect vantage and could hear.

Smurf, knowing my instructions were to involve X-Man in any way possible, decided to forego couth and subtlety to do so. In a certain panic move, his unimaginative ass turned to X-Man himself and explained that his boss, Tee, was hookin' him up with some cash so he could move a little work. He continued with some sob story, saying he had fallen on some hard times with his mama in the hospital and that a yard would really go a long way toward getting his family back on their feet. It was so ridiculous that it was brilliant. X-Man looked over at me. I coolly shrugged my shoulders and nodded.

What happened next would occur in slow-motion action with auditory exclusion, capturing slowly and silently the rewarding culmination of my year-and-a-half of life-altering Fishbowl experiences. X-Man, without hesitation and in the spirit of the glorious day of holy Cripdom he orchestrated, reached into his pocket and handed Smurf the beautiful cocaine that sealed his doom. Although I hoped he would, I still could hardly believe that "Larger-Than-Life" X-Man would even possess such a small amount of dope, let alone sell it like some small time up-and-comer. But that was the beautiful thing about this day. It was ultimate poetic justice. "4x3 Day" would represent the final nail on an operation that would castrate the Crips on the east side of the city. Smurf paid him with my C-note and got into the Benz. We just looked at each other in disbelief as if to say, what just happened? But we were smiling too wide to talk.

That transaction, combined with irrefutable conspiratorial evidence and links from all the other deals and what we would ultimately find upon his arrest (more dope), would seal X-Man's doom. X-Man, nemesis of years past, gang leader, kingpin, and murderer, was finally going to pay his penance.

In all, I had added three more buys that day and bolstered cases on guys I'd already done in, including Deuce and Lil' Saint. I had made all the connections and cases I could. I had solid cases on 51 dope-dealing, gun-selling, and violent-ruling Crips, 41 of whom were slated to be indicted at the federal level. The conspiracy was airtight, and the players were set from top to bottom. It was time.

CHAPTER 16
"Justice, Not Vengeance"

"In certain extreme situations, the law is inadequate. In order to shame its inadequacy, it is necessary to act outside the law. To pursue...natural justice. This is not vengeance. Revenge is not a valid motive, as it's an emotional response. No, not vengeance. Punishment."
-- The Punisher

Coffindaffer called me on my cell.
"Hey, Tegan. Worley and I need to meet with you at his office ASAP.
"OK. What's this about? Something wrong?"
"Just c'mon up here when you get free, and we can fill you in."
"Already on my way. I have a little tidbit for you guys, too."
Mike Worley was the Assistant U.S. Attorney prosecuting my cases in federal court. He and Coffindaffer had been hard at work putting my case files together that passed muster for the feds – which oftentimes is more difficult to get done. Since this was a gang conspiracy case involving confirmed Crip gang members committing feloniousness within their hierarchy, Fishbowl was easy to accept. But there were still several they would eventually leave out of the conspiracy. Those Crips would be charged on the state level.
"Alright, lady and gent. What's the big news?" I asked as I strolled into the U.S. Attorney's office.
"Have a seat, Tegan," Mike said in his ultra-personable tone. "We know you've been at this for a long time. We know you have targets that you still want to hit. We appreciate that you've poured so much of your life into this.
"But…" I said.
But we also want you to know that we will only accept a certain number of defendants in one case. We have to manage our number to ensure success in court and not overextend ourselves.
I knew where they were going with this. I sat silently and listened.
"As much as you want to bring X-Man down as part of this case, it looks like this will be the end of the arrests portion of Operation Fishbowl. You've done a magnificent job and will certainly make the impact you strove to make. But this is where your undercover work ends. It's time you joined us up here at our office and helped us prosecute these guys."
"Well," I said calmly. "I had some great news to share with you guys, too, but…" The feeling this was truly about to end was surreal. I sat in quiet reflection for a moment before sharing my thoughts.

"I appreciate what you two are doing here, too. And I respect you both. I'll admit, this is all quite cathartic for me." I actually felt myself fighting back tears as I spoke. But I took a deep breath and, with a smile, came to. "We nabbed X-Man yesterday."

The line was drawn, and I'd hit the finish line with nary a second to spare. Little did we know that we were in for some of the most trying times yet. It was time for these violent bangers to reimburse the devil with interest. The first trick would be finding all of them when the hammer dropped.

In May of 2006, we got grand jury indictments on all 38 federally charged suspects, with three more to follow. I'd debriefed the "on the books" deals to Coffindaffer so she could properly testify to the grand jury. We decided I would not testify at the grand jury since I would be testifying in the trials. It was less complicated that way, and there would be a greater chance I'd make mental errors if I testified on the same case twice with nearly a year between the two testimonies. The indictments were particularly time-consuming for Coffindaffer and Worley, but they were determined, and I was grateful. So much of this operation now rested in their hands. I was involved in every step and learned a ton, but they certainly led the way.

The indictments were ultimately sealed so that we could plan a roundup in which all the suspects would be arrested at the same time— or, at least, that was the plan. Had the indictments been public, word would have gotten out that a few guys had been picked up on federal warrants. This would pose safety concerns for my informants and me. Also, the remaining bad guys would surely go on the lam, and who knows how long it would take to hunt down all those fools?

We decided to shoot for May 17, 2006, as the roundup date. The preparation for this would prove to be extraordinary, although Coffindaffer was stuck with the brunt of the work since she had the lead on this portion of the operation. We briefed and assigned over 200 local, state and federal law enforcement personnel to capture all 38 suspects (at that time, we still had only the original 38 indictments). The plan would include SWAT teams, Gang Enforcement Tactical teams, K-9 units, interview teams, and evidence specialists. We were slated to roll at 0600 hours on the 17th. That meant everyone would have to be locked and loaded pretty damn early.

Getting that many cops up that early was a feat. Especially when you are talking about the wild cowboy units like SWAT and Gang, who often garner psychotic single people with excitement and late-night-out addiction. Fortunately, at least our Fort Worth units were disciplined and professional above all else, giving me no reason to worry. Who knows how the rest of those federal and state crews lived? Either way, we were set to go. Coffindaffer did the honors of briefing all 200-plus with their assignments while I maintained my low-key status. We had a posse of five from the FBI's Dallas office and an assistant U.S. Attorney up literally all night with us, preparing warrants and printing assignment sheets for the operational plan. I wrote search warrants alongside an attorney while Coffindaffer and her team spent most of the night tweaking the op's plan. The only breaks came when our coffee-filled bladders couldn't hang. It was a grand-scale setup you'd usually only see in the movies, but it was about to get surreal.

I think one of the strangest things about my feelings by this time was that I was about to "come out" and expose my real identity. It was a strange feeling that seemed a mixture of relief, anticipation, and grave concern. I had been through so much since this began. My OTB operations (which still all remained secret at this point), my near nervous breakdowns, my close calls, my surprisingly true friendships, my uniquely enlightening peek into the lives of real people born to unfortunate circumstances, and my near-death experiences, had my emotional compass in a spin. Fortunately for me, there was not one second to ponder any of it. There was so much to do in planning and executing these search and arrest warrants that I didn't sleep a wink for nearly three days leading to the roundup. I didn't sleep on the day of the roundup, either. Try mixing three days of no sleep with some emotional wreckage sometime and see what you feel like. I felt spaced out, but my anxiety was churning out so much adrenaline that I wasn't sleepy. This was a significant moment in Operation Fishbowl, and I was dying to see what happened next.

At 0400 hours on the 17th, I left the U.S. Attorney's office and hauled ass to the house to grab a quick shower before the big dance. Holli was up and waiting with questions and support. During this entire operation, she never went to bed until I arrived home – and she had a real job! Still able to make me smile just by being in the same room, she always brought my crazy undercover mindset to an enjoyable, perspective-laden world I longed to return to soon. Her encouraging words gave me a boost, as did my shower, which was my first in over two-and-a-half days (gross!). Next, I dressed as a proper businessman in an FBI environment, which meant I would be uncomfortable. However, my added personal touch was what I wore underneath. Holli had procured a "Punisher" T-shirt, which I wore under my handsome polyester garb. The Punisher – a Marvel Comics character, if you're not a fan – represented to me a barely controlled crime fighter with little consideration for the bad guys or the means to seek them out. The Punisher was an ex-FBI undercover agent, and although I wasn't really an FBI agent, I felt I could relate under similar circumstances. This day signified the beginning of payback for those who wreaked havoc on our city. I donned the T-shirt with a sense of private, inner pride.

I rushed to get to the command post. I arrived at 0445 hours and immediately began downing coffee like a crackhead in his sixth hour of sobriety. The scene at the command post was surreal. It was a medium-sized room with a long, rectangular conference table in the middle. Along the sides of the table were eight landline phones. All four walls were covered with case-related graphics. One wall had the names and mugshots of every target in Operation Fishbowl. Two others had giant, detailed, color-printed maps of each of the locations, and the entry team's names were assigned to hit each one (this was, of course, pre-Google Maps). The last was a giant dry-erase board where we would soon tally the seizures from each location as each team leader called them in. The room was illuminated by a below-average fluorescent ceiling light that created a hue like an old building, although it smelled new. Cheesy office carpeting and bare white walls stood under the newly hung operational boards.

People assigned to work the command post were beginning to filter in slowly, including the poor, overworked souls who helped us prepare the entire night before. I appreciated them so much for their dedication and told them as much. It's a different experience when you are putting forth that much effort for someone else's project. Too few people would go to these extremes for a cause. This day was proof that there are still hundreds of dedicated folks with true integrity, standards and motivation. They were all putting aside everything to go forth and conquer crime and evil. This was a proud day. The room soon filled to the brink, as did the hallway and standing room outside. Among the crowd were federal ATF, FBI, DEA agents, and others.

As 0555 hours rolled around, I was wired with anticipation and hope. I always got nervous before warrants, not just because of the dangerous nature of the event but also because I hate to lose. The thought of crashing a door and finding nothing after preparing all these officers to risk their lives for the cause always disturbed me. This marked the first time that I wouldn't participate in the serving of my own warrants. As a supervisor and coordinator, I was now left to worry about the safety and success of over 40 tactical assignments.

The arrest teams checked in with the command post one at a time and awaited orders to proceed. Then, the last team called from its staging area, ready to launch. The room fell completely silent for about 30 seconds before 0600. I think I held my breath the entire time. Slow motion entered the scene again as I anticipated the call. Finally, the order came.

"All teams green! All teams green!"

If you have ever seen the old-school Wall Street stock exchange floor in full frenzy, you'd know what the scene here resembled. It was 0-60 in 2.2. Instantly, there was radio chatter from several teams moving into and through their targets. Telephones were ringing off their hooks and the people manning them were shouting questions to Coffindaffer and me. Paperwork once prepped in neat federally styled stacks, was now being strewn about the table. Seemingly random people were being sent on frenzied errands throughout the command post, fetching everything from additional intelligence to additional manpower. All the characteristics of a good day on the stock exchange floor minus the "buy" and "sell" commands. It was undoubtedly one of the most memorable parts of the operation for me.

Soon, arrests were made, and as they were, an X was placed over the corresponding mugshots on the wall; dope and gun seizures were also noted. Several teams hunted their suspects all day, following lead after lead, while others entered the locations we assigned and found their targets immediately.

Finally, a moment of achievement I'd dreamed about for seven years came to fruition. The call came in over the air, and my heart practically stopped. I knew it was coming. The warrant was good. But now it was real!

"Team Charlie. Subject: street name 'X-Man' in custody. Found more dope on him, too."

Not vengeance – Punishment.

By day's end, 26 of my guys had been arrested, along with some dope seizures and 28 guns. With most of these guys facing 20 years to life in federal prison, it was going to be a chore to pick up the rest of the fools we missed now that they knew I was coming. That thought would keep me awake…again.

That afternoon, I was tasked directly by the Chief of Police to compile numbers of arrestees, dope, guns, etc., for the media that we'd collected on the raids. No one was truly ready for this. I did so and sent him the info in an e-mail so he could do the media bidding. Television stations, magazines, and newspapers were clamoring for the story. Coffindaffer, her FBI boss, and one of the veteran Fort Worth Gang Unit sergeants, Bill Beall, handled the news conferences. Even though I had started this ball rolling working under the Narcotics Unit umbrella, the Fort Worth Gang Unit and FBI would share in the credit for Operation Fishbowl. Dozens of others who were also interested in being on TV to take credit for this success jostled for face time.

The story led off the 6 and 10 o'clock newscasts locally, and the police brass hailed it as a major kick in the Crip balls. Coffindaffer, Gang Sgt. Beall, Fort Worth Chief Mendoza, several local and regional police officers, and U.S. Attorney Richard Roper all had their moments in front of the camera. The media ultimately presented it as some long-term gang unit effort and even used 5-year-old footage showing traffic stops in the hood. It was entertaining to watch these new versions of actual events unfold.

'Fishbowl' Sweep Nets 26

May 20--FORT WORTH -- Police say there was no easy way into "The Fishbowl."

The street gang that operated in the neighborhood around Belzise Terrace in east Fort Worth put lookouts at the entrances and exits. If police rolled in, word spread quickly and the crack and heroin being sold in the streets and houses disappeared, police said.

"It has always been a closed neighborhood," said Sgt. Bill Beall of the Fort Worth gang unit. "There are two ways in and out."

"It's been very hard for us to get in there and make cases."

Authorities finally got in, flooding the area Wednesday with more than 200 officers, arresting 26 people and seizing a cache of weapons and an estimated $1 million in drugs. The sweep culminated a 20-month investigation involving federal and local authorities that led to 40 drug trafficking indictments. More arrests are expected soon, officials said.

"Most of the indictments are sealed because the investigation is ongoing," said Jennifer Coffindaffer, special agent with the FBI.

The gang was primarily dealing crack, powder cocaine, and black tar heroin, said Lt. Gene Jones, a police spokesman.

Authorities also served seven search warrants that led to the seizure of $15,000 and 25 assault rifles, sawed-off shotguns, and handguns, said Dale Ensley, special agent for the FBI's Fort Worth-area Safe Streets Task Force. That's almost one gun seized for every person arrested, Ensley said. "They had a tremendous amount of weapons," he said.

The area known as "the Fishbowl" is on the western edge of Cobb Park and is bounded by Colvin Street to the north, Belzise Terrace to the east, Glen Garden Drive to the south and South Riverside Drive to the west.

Beall said the gang was targeted because it was large and well-organized. Some of its members have ties to a family that was involved in the drug trade in that area 20 to 30 years ago, he said. "They have a hierarchy, a leadership involved," Beall said. "They're much more organized than a few people getting together and saying, 'Let's have a gang.'" Beall said he believes that the arrests will reduce the number of shootings and other violent crimes in the city. The most recent homicide in the neighborhood occurred about a month ago, he said.

"They were heavily involved in drugs," he said. "And when you have drugs, you have guns, and you have shootings. Most of the people involved in this had serious criminal records."

Coffindaffer said that, after the evidence was gathered, the arrest sweep took weeks to plan. Officers with the Tarrant County Sheriff's Department, the Dallas division of the Joint Terrorism Task Force and the Fort Worth Police Department narcotics unit and East Division Crime Response Team were among those that participated.

Most of the suspects were arrested Wednesday morning when officers entered the area. One suspect barricaded himself inside a house for about 40 minutes, she said, but surrendered peacefully to the FBI tactical team. A few suspects surrendered Thursday after learning that arrest warrants had been issued for them. The suspects -- all adults -- could face anywhere from five years to life in federal prison if convicted, she said.

The media would remain involved with this for a while, as this was the birth of a new phase in this massive case. My anonymous ass would need some sleep before heading out and hunting the remaining bangers down, but I couldn't afford much. This was getting good, but time was of the essence. I would have to plot ways to get the rest of these punks picked-up before they got to me. And they were organized. That added to the stressful anticipation of how Tee's "friends" would react to learning his true identity.

CHAPTER 17
"Tee's a What?!"

Detention hearings came next. I gave Coffindaffer and Worley complete background packets on each of our arrested suspects. These packets included criminal backgrounds and whatever illegal activities I did with them – on the books, of course. I couldn't disclose my OTB activity since the rules were not followed. When one bends the rules, he cannot leverage the fruits. So, some of these guys would be charged with markedly less than their actual participation dictated, but that was the decision I made for the cause. Regardless, they'd be charged with enough to accomplish what I set out to do. I also couldn't tell Worley or Coffindaffer, or they'd flip out. The feds do not work in gray areas. They are used to working with federally funded projects, teams of professionals, wiretaps, and high-tech equipment to establish their cases. My case was one dude leveraging primitive tactics with not so much as a body wire. It was the only way this could have been accomplished at the time. Leveraging others and going up the chain for wires and gadgets would have blown this op up in a matter of weeks. Besides, the feds only like prosecuting cases that are strong enough to win without question. As long as they didn't know, there would be nothing to question – cuz my arrestees damn sure weren't gonna bring up the fact that there were a bunch of other big deals! The sole purpose of my working OTB was to free myself up to work my way up the ranks and grow my street cred anyway. And for that intent and purpose, it worked perfectly.

The hearings were critical to us since they could determine whether these violent bastards could post a bond and get out. The problems we would face if they were allowed a bond were evident, and the judges agreed. All the bad guys arrested to that point were held with no bond following each hearing. But there were still fugitives out there, and before this got messy, I would have to start looking for them.

By now, everyone had heard about Operation Fishbowl. Although plenty of others were willing to take credit for its success, only a select few were willing to dedicate extra time to fugitive hunting. As it turned out, the same dedicated officers who busted their balls to help me early in the investigation now vowed to help me hunt. Officer Kelly Caruthers, a guy who'd covered my ass dozens of times in the Bowl while I locked myself in these dope dens, was the first to step up. He'd personally tracked and snatched up two of the fugitives already while juggling patrol duties. Impressive.

I teamed up with the U.S. Marshals, and we went hunting all over the region. Traces, phone ruses, fake dope deals, friends-turned-snitches for a few bucks – we used everything we could to get these guys before they could get to me. Word on the street was already out that Tee was a dead man. I began receiving text messages on my cell, threatening my life from people "loosely related" to certain players. We wanted answers, and I was now getting them. This is how they wanted to play it out. I kept my number the same so that I would have the opportunity to at least know from whom and when I was being threatened. I would assume the worst but press on smartly.

I put plans in place to protect us from an attack at my real home, and my wife and son would not sleep there at all for a while unless I were home with them. On numerous occasions, they'd both lay the back seats of my truck down and make little sleeping bag pallets. Then they'd set up a DVD player or video games. They did homework, hung out, talked, watched movies, and eventually slept for the night in my truck while I worked. We presented all of this to my then 11-year-old son as a random opportunity to do something "fun" and hang out later than usual. He seemed to sense something was up but didn't make much of it because he stood to lose the benefits. He was also a star athlete with an insane schedule for a kid his age. This made it easier for him to crash out when it was time. He was mature for his age but was too young for us to share the concept of a threat to him and his family. Overall, it was a temporary solution to an issue that only intensified my resolve to finish this roundup.

After nearly six weeks of hunting fugitives, only GG remained. That concerned me, since he was a proven violent bastard and I needed him locked up yesterday. We busted into his "hideouts" – led to nothing. We questioned his family – he knew we were coming. Finally, he was located, but this location would soon lead to my next cluster screw. And to think, by then I thought there would be no more clusters? Not so much.

On June 28, 2006, at 6:40 a.m., Officer Caruthers called me. He didn't ever need to identify himself. His voice was distinctly country, a tad raspy and low. His laugh would inspire others to join him, regardless of whether what was said was humorous. He was a corn-fed, 6-foot-3, 260-pound, handlebar-mustached ol' country boy. Caruthers was a character indeed. A really good dude. He called my phone.

"Hey, Tegan. I've got this informant over here who says he just saw GG with two other guys inside this house with a bunch of guns and crack on the table."

"Awesome! Where are you? I'll be on my way now!" I proclaimed with both excitement and relief.

He gave me the house's description, address, and information as I headed out. When I arrived, I discovered Caruthers had gone to answer an emergency call, and he had already dropped off his informant. It was most disadvantageous to answer calls working patrol while driving informants around simultaneously. Still, Caruthers came from the gritty Weed and Seed warrant days, where one just figured out ways to make impossible things happen. I called him again from up the street. I described the house the informant had shown him earlier to confirm I was looking at the same one. It was an old brown, frame house built in the 1950s with a poorly kept yard. Caruthers confirmed I was at the right spot when I described a big truck parked in the front yard with four flats and that there were no visible address numbers on the house or curb. That was a typical dope dealer move to change or remove defining address numbers to confuse or cause doubt on the part of the narcs trying to serve a warrant.

"I'll need to talk to your informant to show him a mug shot of GG. You know how my luck runs, man. I need to make sure it's really him in there."

Caruthers assured me that would be difficult since the informant was a transient and had no residence or phone. He was a goner for now.

"Well, is he at least signed up and solidified in the department narc files? You said you'd used him before, right?" I asked Caruthers. If the informant were in our files, I'd be assured he had been proven since it takes several successful deals to prove reliability before being put in our police department's confidential informant files.

Caruthers, whom I obviously trust, assured me the informant was reliable, in our files, and responsible for dozens of successful arrests, search warrants and seizures. Logic and instructions be damned. As far as I was concerned, we were good to go. This dude was gonna kill me or someone else if we didn't hurry.

I decided to start the ball rolling with a little creative thinking. I told Caruthers I decided to write a search warrant for the crack inside the house instead of for GG, based upon the reliable information of his informant, who had proven he was able to correctly ID dope and guns in the past. That way, even if the guy inside were not GG, we'd be there legally to seize the dope and guns inside, anyway. Sure, it would be great to send the informant inside to buy crack and then test it to make sure the information was good, and that GG was the guy in the mug shot, but this was an exigent circumstance. We believed we had a certified violent gang member with a past attempted murder charge and a current federal felony warrant for his role in Operation Fishbowl inside the house at that very moment. So, I made haste - not waste.

Since there had been a few minutes between Caruthers leaving the house and my arrival, I told Caruthers to at least try to find his informant again. If he found him, I told him to have him go by the house one more time and see if GG was still inside. Meanwhile, I left to write the warrant and ask a judge to sign off on it.

When I got back, I talked to Caruthers again. He'd found the informant and sent him back to the house and confirmed GG was still inside with the dope, guns and the two other dudes. The only difference this time was that somehow, they all knew that the cops were outside. The newest problem was that Caruthers and the few officers he had collected to help him while I was away didn't see the informant actually go inside the house from where they watched. They only saw him go to the side of the house. The informant told them that he'd gone in through a side door, and Caruthers reassured me that the informant had pointed out the exact house to him earlier. Neither of us had any real concerns at that point other than that we now faced a potential shootout situation since we were made. That was just one of the consequences for Caruthers having to work an informant out of a marked police unit.

I called SWAT to execute the warrant because of the dangerous circumstances and lack of help this early in the day. I met with the SWAT commander and briefed the details, and they prepared the entry plan. They'd run warrants there six times before, so they already had the floor plans, past tenants, and arrestees in their files. However, they did not want to take an unnecessary risk by entering immediately when the bad guy suspected the police were coming and could be prepared to ambush them. So, they planned to use a different strategy from the norm. I was stuck in a mobile command post around the corner from the target, praying for safety and success…once again. I was beginning to miss kicking doors.

.

I sat in nervous anticipation as I heard the teams were about to round the corner. I watched from the safe vantage of the command post truck as SWAT's armored vehicle pulled in front of the house and stopped. Officers quickly bailed out and surrounded it. They called over the loudspeaker for GG to come out with his hands up. Over and over, the commands were given with no response. I was beginning to worry. Finally, they decided to shoot tear gas into the house. One by one, canisters of tear gas were launched into the house through the windows. Soon, there were six, then seven, then eight, then nine canisters of tear gas spent; No one came out. The team, donning gas masks, decided it was time to go in after GG.

My mind was spinning. There was no way he was still in there with that much tear gas. Even Superman would be choking to death. As the SWAT team rushed the house, an intuitively sinking feeling came over me. Was this the right house? I was positive that it was the house Caruthers described, but…

Soon enough, I received my answer. The SWAT team emerged from the clearing gas, defeated, empty-handed, and just in time to greet the media and neighbors who'd gathered across the way to watch this embarrassing crime drama unfold. The house was destroyed. The flash-bangs and gas had left broken windows, burns, and stench; the door and frame were splintered, all in addition to the fact that it was barely livable to begin with. The homeowner had also arrived by then and was already interviewing with the media outside. Despite this being a recent dope house where SWAT had successfully hit and confiscated contraband, he would present as a totally innocent person being victimized. This would be 100% my fault.

Anything "Fishbowl" was attracting major news coverage, which was no different, except that this news was bad. If my heart could sink any lower, it did then. I sifted through the crowd in a full-faced mask and found Caruthers. I told him I had to talk to this so-called informant in person and to call me when he found him. I was gonna be in deep doo-doo.

A few hours later, Caruthers called. He'd found the informant, the same informant who had proven himself dozens of times to be reliable, the same informant who was signed up in the files with the police department, the same informant who had nothing to gain by misleading us since he would only be paid if GG were caught. We, along with another officer and Caruthers's supervisor, met with the informant at the police station so I could interview him. I introduced myself and began by telling him to give me specific driving directions to the house he'd seen GG in earlier that morning.

This informant was a slightly older cat in his 50s with dark, weathered skin and rotted teeth. He was slovenly dressed, and I'd have bet my house he hadn't showered in a week. He had to know something was up when he was dragged in here to talk with all of us, especially after witnessing the debacle at the house he'd sent us to. He hesitated a moment and then recited directions to our target:

"You take Berry Street, then go south to the dead end. Then you kinda loop to the right and go to Rufus. Turn to the left, and it's like the 4th or 5th house down on the right. I think the address is like 3-6-1-6 or 3-6-1-7."

The hair on the back of my neck stood up. The investigator in all of us, I was certain, sensed the same thing, but I went ahead and asked the inevitable: "Why do you think it's one of those addresses?"

"Cuz the numbers is over the front door."

Gasps echoed about the room, Caruthers barked an uninterpretable expletive, and then the room fell dead silent. I looked at the "informant" who now looked like someone standing on the wrong side of a firing line.

"This interview is over," I said, knowing Internal Affairs would probably finish it later. Caruthers' informant was mistaken. Our house had no numbers displayed at all. We had just raided the wrong house.

The informant pointed to the house with Caruthers that morning as they drove by it in the patrol car. However, the informant was so concerned with being seen inside a passing police unit that he'd pointed to the wrong house and confirmed the location that would soon burn me and everyone else associated with this debacle. I trusted Caruthers, Caruthers trusted the informant, SWAT trusted me, and Caruthers's supervisor trusted all of us. Meanwhile, the informant was a moron and took all of us down with him.

What's way worse, our SWAT officers could have all easily been killed since we suspected the real house was likely next door to the one that we hit. GG probably watched the whole thing from a front-row seat and laughed. But as we all know, it's not who laughs first that's important.

Ultimately, the story would be plastered all over local media outlets and broadcast nationally on the Fox News Channel. The Fort Worth Police Department would be embarrassed, and Caruthers and I would face disciplinary action. We would ultimately emerge with a mere slap on the wrist, but it still caused me public humiliation. It also brought more determination to catch GG and give him what he deserved.

Humility is good for the soul. And what better way to demonstrate humility than to allow yourself to be humiliated in front of your peers nationwide? I lacked any recognition for Operation Fishbowl at all at that point, and now I got to stand and be chastised for this moronic event.

However, when someone works as hard as Caruthers, especially when the work is done for the cause and not for personal glory, unfortunate events like this come with the territory. There are far too few rewards to counter the bad stuff that happens during a career of aggressive work ethic. Some officers I've seen become lazy and complacent because they know you can't get in big trouble for working the minimum requirement. Meanwhile, the hard workers with 100 successes for every failure will receive little to no reward and receive days off without pay for that one screw-up. Make no mistake, this was definitely a screw-up, but this kind of incident never happens to the worthless cop who parks his police car under a tree and reads the paper all day. Eventually, I got a tip from an old informant of mine and I passed it to my brothers in the Gang Unit to handle it their way. They swooped in and arrested GG without incident. It was certainly an anti-climactic close to a manhunt that had caused such a ruckus! But success and survival for the good guys prevailed.

GG would refuse to speak with me, Coffindaffer, Worley or anyone else who could possibly help him in any way. He pled "not guilty" and took his cases to trial. There, he and his attorney used a strategy to try and discredit me by bringing up the "wrong house incident." They hoped a jury would find me unreliable and irresponsible and therefore not believe I did any of the hand-to-hand deals with this jackass. It didn't work. The trial lasted one short day and the jury came back with a unanimous guilty verdict on all counts, including trafficking and conspiracy. GG was sentenced to 60 years in federal prison with no chance of parole—last laugh.

It's tragic to see someone that young take that road, but the people who make true sacrifices to do things the right way deserve to have people like GG gone. I was proud and relieved to know there would be one less violent banger on the streets, and that the "wrong house incident" ultimately culminated to a success story.

While that drama unfolded and the arrestees were held without bond, Coffindaffer and I interviewed many of them, trying to get cooperation, information, a plea, or all of the above.

This posed a fascinating dilemma for me with a lot of these guys. Although the objective was to get them off the streets for as long as possible, some were cool with me at one time. I'd spent more time hanging out with some of these fools than I did wheeling and dealing. After all, once you've shared a 40 oz. and a game of Madden, haven't you male-bonded in some way?

To be honest, I truly liked a couple of these guys. Some I even considered friends. I felt they could change their ways with proper guidance and help. I had no way of knowing how they'd react when they saw me for the first time as a cop. I did, however, hope that the select few might cooperate so I could testify on their behalf and ask for a lighter sentence. It was the noble thing to do for those that intuitively struck me as having the most potential for positive change. Others I liked but worried they would return to crime the second they were released.

I was stressed as hell about this whole "Tee exposes himself as a cop" bombshell as we launched into our interviews. The first post-arrest meeting was scheduled with Zule, the linebacking, gangbanging, dope-runner from Poly. Coffindaffer and I were entering the interview room inside the prison to wait for Zule's attorney to show up. Just then, we realized Coffindaffer had forgotten some documents we needed for the interview. At the same time, the guard had arrived with Zule, all 6-foot-3, 260 pounds of him, and Coffindaffer politely asked if she could use the fax machine to retrieve the documents we needed. Before anyone thought better of it, the guard unshackled and released Zule into the room with me. He locked the door from the outside, and he and Coffindaffer took off in search of the ever-important fax machine.

So, there we stood together, inside a conference room with no guard, mano-a-mano, and waiting for Zule's attorney to arrive, for the guard to return, or for the much-anticipated throwdown. The situation was so ironic it fascinated me. Perhaps he felt the same way? I thought this would be an awesome fight if it came down to it. It wouldn't be personal to me, but our caveman brains would probably both enjoy the experience. I was intrigued but on guard. As we looked at one another, I watched his face slowly morph from total surprise to disbelief and finally to acceptance. The sad look of concession said it all. He'd been had. He stepped back, looked down to the floor and shook his head violently as if to try and expunge what he'd just seen from his mind.

I made the first move. After an uncomfortable silence passed, I extended my hand to him. "Nothing personal, Zule."

He quietly returned a shake, then spoke softly, curious:

"Man, I dunno what to say, Tee. How you get all the way in this, man? We had bidness runnin'. Now what?"

"Man, what's up now is that we have to concentrate on our new business, important business – business that could mean everything to your family now, bro. Think about your family."

We spoke for several minutes before Coffindaffer and the attorney arrived. We talked about his kids, his wife and his safety. Zule was a good dude to talk to, but he also faced charges from the state in addition to ours for shooting two rival gangbangers who both lived to tell. That kind of stuff said to me he needed to stay locked up at least a little while. He'd lived the gang life many only pretended to live.

The next interview was with Kendrick. We spent a decent amount of time together out in the street, and I discovered that a first impression is hard to break. Coffindaffer and I arrived at the federal holding facility and made our way to an old, cramped interview room. We found Kendrick seated at a lone table in the center. We set our notebooks, recorders, and pens down, then sat directly across from him. I instinctively reached over the table and greeted him with a street-standard shake.

"Sup, Ken?" I said.

"Whatcha know good, Tee?" he calmly replied.

I sat as Coffindaffer opened the interview and explained what we were there to accomplish.

"Hello, Mr. Kendrick. I'm Special Agent Coffindaffer with the Federal Bureau of Investigation, and this is Officer Tegan Broadwater of the Fort Worth Police Department." His eyes remained fixated on her this whole time. I wondered if he'd even heard what she just said.

"You have gotten yourself into a bad situation here. According to the federal guidelines in your case, you are potentially looking at a 30-year sentence. We are here to debrief your personal and criminal history and try to understand what got you to this point. Furthermore, I want you to understand that the government insists that you be completely truthful, or there will not be an opportunity for you to reduce your sentence." She framed his dilemma in no uncertain terms and let him know that absolute transparency might earn him some grace from the judge. She was on a roll, so I let her do her thing and just listened.

They talked about where he grew up and about the first time he was exposed to gang life. He was pretty talkative, but the subject matter consisted of mere softballs at that point. As she dug deeper and deeper into his criminal activity, he became less forthcoming, and we knew it. All the while, he stared straight at her, focusing on her motive and trying to anticipate where the questions would lead. Of course, she was good, and there was no way he'd guess. So, the more she prodded him, the more agitated he became. She called him out for lying since she knew his true history from me, and she kept correcting him to demonstrate she knew more than he thought. She was growing impatient now, too.

"Kendrick, you are lying", she barked. "You were a distributor, not just some user. And you did contribute to the Polywood and 4x3 Crip organization. Don't you wonder how we know where you got your kilos?"

Kendrick was not having it. He was done with this accusatory rant. He finally turned to look at me for the first time since we'd greeted.

"Tee! Tell her, man! You know I wasn't out bangin' wit dem fools! Tell her! You know this, fam!"

I was caught off guard. Ken still viewed me as Tee from the street, not Officer from the police department. He held animosity for Coffindaffer, whom he now considered the face that locked him up but couldn't envision me any other way but Tee. Not only that, but he was also now asking me to lie for him!

"Bro, listen to me. She is shooting you straight. You need to tell her everything, bro. Think about your family. They need you. Hell, I want you to get out soon so you can prove to all these bastards you're capable of greater things."

I liked Kendrick. I really liked Kendrick, in fact. But he had a long history of getting out of prison and returning to the game. What was worse, he didn't believe me. Not that I blame him, mind you. I was also freakin' nuts to think that me telling him I was really a cop but to trust me for real this time would work. It was a frustrating position to be in because I really did mean what I said. But, with no other options, he became desperate.

"Man, you mothafuckas just tryin' ta frame me cuz I'm black, and that's some bullshit!"

I immediately shot him an austere look that had to say it all, because I wasn't about to entertain that nonsense. I had to remind myself these guys would not all come through like I'd hoped they would.

I went through dozens of interviews and got mixed reactions. I went in to each one with excited anticipation and intrigue. They were experiences I could get nowhere else. I had fascinating interviews with Tre, Cuda, Candy and D from the Bowl. Some of the Poly guys were great, too. Deuce admitted plotting with Tre to murder Stick before he was incarcerated.

In what should have been the dream interview, X-Man's visit was lame. I'd spent so many exhausting years of my career hunting him, and I expected a fiery ending to such a dramatic build. His dominance over the hoods here left so much destruction in its wake, yet he seemed to exit with a whimper. I suppose it was ironic in some ways. As X-Man, the ruthless gang leader who seemed to bow out peacefully, remained conspicuously quiet, the whole city was a safer, quieter place. He denied so much it was hard to take any good info from the meetings. But he was going to fry. He was looking at four new murder cases that surfaced during other interviews of those who would talk.

Additionally, and much like Deuce and Phat, he couldn't deny his gang ties. He hailed the Crip life as if his mother's life depended on it. It just amazed me. I figured that although this interview seemed anti-climactic, the real time to be excited would be his sentencing. I couldn't wait.

However, none fascinated me more than my interview with Nasty. He had been X-Man's hands-on VP, moving $250,000 worth of cocaine per week for his mentor. We actually sat for hours on end as he told me his story. This was particularly fascinating since I was so involved in much of the history he talked about. He mentioned all the dope houses he ran that I had hit with Weed and Seed A-Teams and Narcotics units. He was candid about the things I missed and where all his money had gone. His women, his children, his gang life, his dope; it was like spending seven years on an intricate 5000-piece puzzle and discovering at the end that you are short pieces. Then a guy like Nasty comes in and not only supplies you with the missing pieces but puts them in place for you. He talked about his gambling habit. He'd sometimes gamble up to a half-million dollars over a weekend. He'd be rich if he had been more responsible with his money like X-Man. He sat in his living room one time and spent all day and night hand-counting 15 million dollars, and now he had zip. I was riveted through the entire interview; I felt my years of work culminated in this one sitting.

Nasty fully cooperated. We asked a lot of him, including testimony in court in exchange for a break on his sentence. He'd been arrested and sent to prison before the other Fishbowl conspirators for beating up his wife for the third time. He handed most of his business down to his little brother, Big Killa. Although aptly named, Big Killa was nothing like his mild-mannered bro. He was an absolute ass – a punk kid with a lot to prove to people who expected him to live up to his brother's legacy. Knowing Killa was a Polywood Crip, I had scored a load of coke and a Mac-10 from him, which sealed his fate.

Big Killa insisted on going to trial, much like GG. He was also facing a murder charge for killing an innocent 14-year-old boy with a stray bullet during a gang shootout in Poly a year earlier. I asked Nasty if he wanted to testify against his brother, but after thinking about it, he respectfully declined. I understood. Testifying on some bad dude who doesn't care about you unless you're paying him to save yourself is one thing. Family honor is another. Besides, we could slam dunk Big Killa without additional help, anyway.

For his substantial assistance to the government, Nasty was sentenced to a measly 20 years without parole. This was after he faced a possible life sentence for his kingpin role, which is looked upon quite seriously at this level.

Big Killa's results were markedly different. His insistence on testifying was his undoing. He was an annoying thug, and it showed on the stand. He was a liar and it showed on the stand. He was a moron, gangbanging, murdering, dope slinging and gun-toting loser with no social redeeming value for our protected public – and it showed on the stand. Big Killa received life plus five years in federal prison without parole for his role in Operation Fishbowl and was still waiting for his murder trial to begin.

The interviews, pleas, and trials continued for an entire year. Though the workload was still outrageous, it was starting to feel good to be me again. But the next phase proved that I must always be prepared for new and wonderfully stressful experiences.

CHAPTER 18
"Trials and The Fab 41"

We only went to trial on seven guys but prepared for several others before they decided at the last minute to plead guilty. Most of the Fishbowl defendants were assigned public defenders – which can be hit or miss regarding performance. With luck, one might be appointed a fantastic lawyer to take their case. One that is passionate about their work and that has their client's best interest in mind, even if it means more work for less money. Conversely, there are also sleazy ones who refuse to entertain the possibility that their client could ever be guilty, thereby creating an ill-advised strategy that only hurts that client in the end. The issue is that when one elects to have an attorney appointed, they do not get to choose. The ones that could choose in this case, were the big-money bangers that could afford big-money attorneys. But even the big-money attorneys recognized the massive hill they'd have to climb to beat these cases. The only way they could succeed in trial would be to attack my integrity – which would prove futile. So, the remaining suspects pled guilty, knowing that, based on having dealt with me first-hand, they were screwed. Now they were faced with the decision to either cooperate for possible leniency or "roll the dice" and let a federal judge decide their fate sans a lick of help.

The first guy to be sentenced was Tre. He pled guilty, drew a "tough-on-crime" judge, the Honorable Judge John H. McBryde, and was given 20 years with no parole. When he was sentenced, the newspapers and television newscasts were buzzing and so was the jail. Everyone I'd locked up was holding their breath to see if we were bluffing about how much time they were looking at. When Tre got 20 years after rumors swirled that he did cooperate with us, they flipped out.

Phat was the worst, going nuts inside and threatening the lives of several people who were cooperating with us to help themselves. Phat had a lot of pull on the street, and it spilled over into the jail. He'd even conned a crooked guard into delivering notes and verbal messages to Cuda, Tre, G-Pacc, Candy, and others. These messages threatened their lives and the safety of their families. Phone calls were made to the families of our cooperators by friends and family members of Phat's as well. He ultimately forced them to write, sign, and notarize letters saying that everything they had told the feds about him was a lie. These intimidated souls also did so without their attorney's knowledge. He was screwing himself and screwing, even worse, those that were really trying to help. It was the way of the Phat.

This posed a dilemma on multiple levels. First, anyone writing and signing such a letter discredited himself as a witness on the stand and now faced full punishment without a once-promising break from the government. Second, we had a corrupt asshole prison guard to investigate. Third, we now had to create separation orders for many of the arrestees and put Phat into "seg" (isolation) to keep his threats to a minimum. Unfortunately, separating this many people proved nearly cataclysmic. Only a few local jail facilities could house the Fab 41 and their ten state stepchildren. The environment was out of control in most of them, mixing the cooperators with the "I ain't snitchin'" group who were hammered most extraordinarily at trial. The fights, the threats, the separation orders, the corrupt guards, the supposed sworn documents and the threats on the family members kept the few remaining hours in our days saturated with juicy drama.

G-Pacc took a disappointing hit from this movement. He was easily one of the most charismatic and endearing guys in the whole op. He always had Tee's back but was also the type with a track record of returning to a life of crime. He had spent most of his adult and juvenile life behind bars. He was intelligent and well-spoken but had an unfortunate past. Notably, Worley had prosecuted the man who assaulted G-Pacc decades earlier. Now here sat G-Pacc, an abused soul manifested in gang life and who couldn't fend off his demons. This case uncovered yet another sad and ironic story. My perspective and determination to contribute to those like Pacc grew as I learned of his past. I rooted for him. He had something to offer. I just didn't know what yet.

Pacc pled guilty. After signing the bogus paperwork for Phat, the manipulative bully, Pacc's chances for leniency were dissolved. He'd discredited himself as a useful witness and would never be given a chance to testify and preserve what was left of his free life. He ended up sentenced to 40 years in federal prison with no parole for his role in Operation Fishbowl, but he was on parole, too. Once the state revoked his parole, he'd have to complete that 27-year Aggravated Robbery sentence before he could even start his fed time. G-Pacc may die in prison, and that saddens me. We may never know what we're missing.

Just before he received his sentence, the judge asked him if he had anything to say. His words illustrated his intelligence, his sense of humor, his guilt, and the reason I couldn't help but really like him:

Yes, sir. First, I would like to apologize to the court for taking up your time. And, Mr. Worley, the prosecutor, I apologize to you. And of course (he turned to look at me) even to 'Tee,' who's a pretty good undercover agent. It's pretty hard to fool ol' Pacc, but you did it.

Your Honor, when I first went to prison, digital watches was a new thing. I'm trying to express here how long I've been involved in this type of thing. It always had something to do with drugs even though some of my past has been violent crimes. I never got a chance to even see a microwave oven work until 1990. I think about that a lot, and I mean, it saddens me. I don't know how it makes anyone else feel, and I'm not doing this to make anybody feel bad for me. Don't woe me. Don't pity me.

Here recently, I think it may have been somewhere around 2000, I was working a trash detail in prison, and I found this object, a little pink deal. I thought it was a lady's compact that has a little mirror and a little powder deal in it. I opened it up, and it turned out to be a calculator...what I thought was a calculator. I tried to add on it, and some numbers came across the screen. It turned out to be a cell phone. I'd never seen a cell phone. I'd only heard of these things.

I'm only saying this to give you a more comprehensive understanding, which would better qualify your opinion of me. I've been in prison so long, there are things out here in this world I don't even know about, and I hope that maybe one day I may get a chance to see these. Here recently, I saw a commercial on TV where a man had a car park itself.

So, you know what I am asking for here is not mercy or leniency. But I am asking that you mitigate the severity of this punishment because I'd like to make it back to this world again before they start flying cars."

Stick's decision to be one of the seven to take us to trial also proved interesting. He lost, of course, but as I stared at his smug expression, I couldn't stop thinking about little Cedric, whose father Stick murdered. I still saw Cedric fairly often, and I considered it fortunate that his father was killed while he was very young. He'd grow up without a father but wouldn't have to live with the grief and devastation a younger man might experience with a father's murder. Stick denied everything, and he paid the price for it. While he waited for his two murder trials, the judge hammered ol' Stick, sentencing him to 30 years in federal prison without parole for his role in Operation Fishbowl. This is certainly the kind of guy who needed to go away for good. His punishment meant everyone was safer and my work was worth it.

His girlfriend doesn't think so, however. She had no idea what kind of man Stick was, despite the police reports that described how Stick had kidnapped her and her baby and then beat her senselessly. She frequently sent threatening text messages to my cell phone. I let her so she could get it all out of her system. Plus, it allowed me to remain keenly aware of the new potential threats my family and I faced. It was better to stay in the know, even if what I knew was bad. Perhaps all her common sense was beaten out of her long ago, but all I could do was watch my back, hope she found a decent guy, finally realize what an abusive loser Stick is, and move on.

Razor, the dude who vouched for me at the X-Man Crip Day transaction, took us to trial and actually made a decent run. He managed to skate the charges for the dope that was confiscated at his house during the roundup but still got hammered for the deliveries to me, as well as the conspiracy charges. During a search of Lil' Saint's incoming jail mail, we discovered an anonymous handwritten plot, complete with drawings depicting the murders of Worley, Coffindaffer, and me. His notes included a courtroom layout, dates, seating arrangements, and the times we'd be there. After thoroughly investigating the notes, we determined Razor was the author. The first thing we did was let the judge know about it. Security was beefed up for his sentencing. All went smoothly since his plot with Lil' Saint had been foiled. His trial ended without incident – unless you count the sentence of 15 years in federal prison without parole for doing business with Tee, an incident.

Razor gave me deathly glares throughout his trial and sentencing. Following his guilty verdict, he was cuffed and escorted out of the courtroom and passed right in front of my chair. As he walked by, he glared at me with pent-up spite, pissed.

"Click-clack, motherfucker," he muttered to me as if he were chambering a round in his SKS.

I recalled some lyrics he'd written that we seized from his house during our roundup. We'd included them with our exhibits at his trial to show his gang affiliation. His lovely poetry about Spring flowers read:

"Banging"
[Chorus] "Banging-Banging" tha funk (nigga)

From day one tha place were I was born in Funky Town, "Fort Worth Tx" were I was raised in tha city were you can come up a Gaddy - You either make it or fold like cards, It's do or die situation, life on tha edge Trying to get that bread and be feeded, Staying on top is what wes tried for, sometimes we fall down, an hard getting back up.

[Chorus] "Banging-Banging" tha funk (nigga)

My niggaz don't give a fuck, if it's your last buck – yo - on a nigga but coin run on luck time cuz I need anotha buck – What you know about thas gangs No I'm not w/anger what the hell you think a Nigga stayin in the streets all night long, with a cash sock mann I'm get it gone – that every cuzz be holden motherfucker zone, two shots click clack an now you gone – fuck you didn't know click clack!

I looked up at him calmly.
"More like 'clink-clank' for you." Those prison doors will remind him of me every day.

Kendrick pled guilty, but his sentencing was one of the more fascinating courtroom experiences. He and his attorney brought family, friends, and a room full of kids to testify on his behalf. They each explained his dedication to his three children and that he was a peewee football coach.

"If he goes to prison, his football kids would be devastated," his mother whined.

When I heard this, I became so angry that I literally broke a sweat. I knew first-hand what it meant to be a peewee football coach myself. It can be one of the more important mentoring roles one can play in a young man's life. It sickened me that he, among others like Phat and Cuda, purported themselves as leaders and role models to children while they raped, shot, and sold dope for a living. Fortunately for me, the Honorable Judge Terry Means held the same sentiment:

Coach gets 10 years in drug case

Someday, U.S. District Judge Terry Means said Monday, the boys coached by Kendrick will be fathers. They may entrust their children's well-being to a youth football coach like Kendrick. And he said he hopes they will not feel cynical about the value of role models. Means sentenced Kendrick Williams, 32, to 10 years in federal prison Monday morning after he pleaded guilty. He was among the people indicted in the Operation Fishbowl crackdown on cocaine distribution in southeast Fort Worth. Prosecutors noted that the quantities Kendrick sold were larger than what ordinary street-level dealers sell. More disheartening, however, is the knowledge that Kendrick's double life means a drug dealer garnered the respect and loyalty of the neighborhood children as a coach, Means said. "I don't think there's any title more respectful than coach," said Means, who, away from court, has also been active in youth sports. With sadness and disappointment in the air, Kendrick turned to family and friends and tearfully apologized. Earlier in the morning, Means sentenced another defendant, who went by the street name "Stick," 22, to 20 years in federal prison for his part in the drug distribution trade in the neighborhood known to law enforcement officers as the Fishbowl.

Cuda actually helped us out quite a bit. He was planning to plead guilty and take his lumps before he witnessed Coffindaffer taking the stand to support one of our other cooperating defendants. This guy had helped us greatly, and she went to bat for him. His sentence was reduced from 20 years to six because of what she said. Cuda witnessed this first-hand while he waited his turn for sentencing. After she'd finished and it was his turn, Cuda spoke to his attorney who convinced Worley and the judge to delay his sentencing so he could debrief again and fully cooperate. Cuda wanted a reduced sentence like this other dude had just received. He was looking at a probable 27-year sentence at the time.

We spoke with Cuda several times, and he was a great interview. He was a guy I really liked both in jail and when we dealt on the streets. He was laid-back and easy to talk to, but most importantly, Cuda was the only person in my case who had to be arrested during our roundup from an actual job. At the time of the roundup, he had been trying to get out of the game for a while before being picked up on the Fishbowl charges and was doing well.

I had high hopes for Cuda. He had worked closely with Phat, whom I obviously did not like, and he had information about Phat that would ultimately help convince Phat to plead guilty to his charges. I would take this tradeoff all day long: time off Cuda's sentence in exchange for hammering Phat.

Cuda was sentenced to a measly ten years for his part in the Fishbowl Crip conspiracy. After he received his sentence, I walked up to him and shook his hand as he spoke.

"We straight?"

"Yeah, we straight," I replied.

I was glad he got a break. I still pray that he will be one to get out and be a productive member of society. He'd shown some promise once before, so he could do it again.

Of all the breaks handed out by the great judges, Candy got one of the biggest. She'd been truly remorseful and honest from the beginning. I also felt bad for her family, who, when she was arrested, took on all three of her children, including a one-year-old fathered by Tre. It's so sad when I take out a mother and a father, but Candy would be out soon enough.

I testified at her sentencing and expressed my belief that she was honest and had been extremely helpful to us. I also mentioned that she'd acted as a mere middle[wo]man when working with me on the streets. She received only two years out of the 20 that had been recommended before she agreed to cooperate. In the interim, Holli and I provided financial and emotional support to Candy's sister, who was a single mother with children of her own, and Candy's mother, who had debilitating heart problems and couldn't work. They are genuinely dedicated to the kids' well-being and are battling the odds to keep moving in the right direction. Bless 'em.

Then came the fateful day that represented the culmination of my undercover adventure. X-Man, ultimate nemesis, entered a plea agreement with us for a sentence not to exceed 20 years. We only agreed to this because he still faced four other state murder charges for whacking those rival gangbangers. From the hundreds of interviews Coffindaffer and I conducted, nine cold-case murders were solved. What a person facing over a 30-year sentence will tell you to whittle away some of that time is incredible. Thankfully, X-Man was brought up during some of those salvation-inspired regurgitations.

Everyone was terrified to say anything about X-Man at first. The attitudes slowly changed once the sentences began pouring in and everyone realized that people were getting slammed with massive jail time. X-Man was not only a significantly notable Crip gang leader with ties to his South-Central LA constituents; he was a true player of the game. He was not afraid to murder, and that became obvious once people started presenting evidence and information to that effect. X-Man had so much money and power that his physical stature had little bearing on others' perception of him. He was a dark, merely medium-built, pony-tailed, gang-tatted dude, but he was baaad. I was proud to see X-Man go down. It had been a long time coming. For seven years I'd pursued him. Upon his sentencing of 20 years, I thanked God for seeing to it that I survived X-Man's hunt and capture. I was beginning to feel like God's favorite kitty cat.

Meanwhile, after his arrest, X-Man's wife, Reetha, had been trying to take over his business. She'd been with him through thick and thin. Reetha was petite, once pretty, and light-skinned with scattered tatts and a tattered past. Her status was established only because she'd been with the king so long. Now that he was locked up, her status became one of a fish out of water, an easy target. She had no business trying to jump into a game so brutal and large. Hundreds of thousands of dollars changed hands every week between veterans of the vicious street survival game. I knew there was no way she could maintain, and I figured when I completed this trial mess, I'd track her and try to snag and tag X-Man's stash of millions I knew he had hidden somewhere.

However, tragedy struck in the darkest way. No more than a week after X-Man was sentenced, Reetha was assassinated at an Arlington, Texas, nightclub parking lot by a Blood. It's sad to see the perpetual evil in this game, but it is in the rules when you sign up to play. I can only imagine what must have been going through X-Man's mind after that week of events, but I do know that there is no doubt we are better and safer without him.

FORT WORTH

Police are looking for the gunman who fatally shot a Fort Worth woman as she sat in the passenger seat of a car as it left a north Arlington nightclub early Sunday, authorities said. Reetha Parker, 23, died at 1:15 p.m. Sunday at John Peter Smith Hospital in Fort Worth, according to the Tarrant County medical examiner. Witnesses told police that Parker was involved in a "physical altercation" with another woman inside the After Life Club in the 2600 block of Avenue E East, police spokeswoman Christy Gilfour said.

"Shortly afterward, the victim was in the passenger seat of a Chevy Suburban that was leaving the club when a man walked up to the vehicle and fired several rounds from a handgun," Gilfour said in a news release. "Witnesses described the shooter as a black man in his mid-to-late 20s who is 5 feet 8 inches tall with a thin build, wearing glasses, a black baseball cap, and a black jacket," she said. "The suspect and a passenger were observed leaving the scene in a red car, possibly a Chevrolet Impala," she said.

The Fab 41 and their ten steps were all convicted. Not one skated. The effects can only be measured once time tells. However, the direct and immediate positive impact on the neighborhoods and the freed innocents who live in them has shown how rewarding Operation Fishbowl was and hopefully will be for years to come. I will never be the same. My faith is forever strengthened, and my true love and appreciation for my family and my freedom solidified. I now hope for continued change for the better, but there is still much to do.

CHAPTER 19
"The Greatest Reward"

With fall in full swing, the capricious Texas weather was reasonable, and people spent more time outside. It was mid-October 2007, and most of the smoke and destruction of Operation Fishbowl had dissipated. I had been near the Bowl since the operation ended, but not in the Bowl. I knew that to have closure, I'd have to somehow peek into the lives of the innocent, hard-working people who remained. After all, they inspired my launching of Operation Fishbowl in the first place. But I was privately worried. What if it had returned to its crime-laden form? What if no one felt safe? What if children were still unable to play outside or walk to school? What if I'd done all this for nothing?

I hopped in a piece of crap, stripped out, 8-year-old Ford Focus with bicycle wheels and dark, tinted windows that the Gang Unit kindly provided my now uncelebrated ass, and headed that way. The trip over felt different. I was by myself and started rolling the windows down out of habit as I approached the Bowl. I used to do this to hear the bad guys talking around me better, and they could see who I was as I drove in. I laughed inside when I caught myself doing it, but I kept them down, anyway.

I decided to enter via the west entrance first. As I entered, the first thing I saw was a Hispanic family hanging out on their patio. They had lived there for about five years next to LP's old west-entrance lookout house, which is now vacant. Just a year ago, KiKi had been murdered in their front yard. I stopped and talked to them.

"Hello, ma'am; I'm doing a follow-up report on the police operation and the raids that went down here last year. May I ask you a few questions?" I showed them my badge.

"Oh, si, you to speak to my daughter," the elderly woman told me with a heavy accent. She didn't speak English well, so I looked to the daughter, who was about 25 years old, of average height, poor, but obviously a determined soul.

"Have you noticed a difference in the neighborhood since last year's police raids?"

"Yes, sir. It used to be real, real, bad here. My mom would call the police every single day to complain about the drugs and the prostitutes all around us, but she couldn't leave her name - you know what I mean? It was all day and night, but now it's so much better." She turned to her mother, and they briefly spoke to each other in Spanish. "I mean, every once in a while, we might see a prostitute near the corner by the motel, but my mom hasn't had to call in a long time for anything."

Her answer filled my heart with hope, but I purposefully remained cautiously optimistic. I thanked them and drove on down toward the next corner. On the way, I saw two families outside well-kept homes. Their kids were outside playing together. This would have been considered an absolute anomaly in this hood's historical criminal past. It was absolutely amazing to see. The only other time I used to see kids around was immediately after school, but even then, they usually stayed inside or played somewhere safer.

I reached the corner house and remembered a call I'd answered there eight years prior as I spotted the mother outside. An older guy I didn't recognize was working on a car in the driveway. The house didn't look improved, but the same tenants were there, so I couldn't expect much. By the time we'd taken down LP's, the gang leader, he'd already moved a few blocks out of the Bowl anyway. His more recent house was now fixed up and re-rented. At least he was gone.

I made the corner and came to Phat's old house. It had burned halfway to the ground and was boarded up. Dilapidated and musty, it sat in agony, waiting for someone to condemn it and put it out of its misery. Inside, there were remnants of Phat's operations and personal belongings. Old pictures of guys throwing up gang signs, pots and pans used for crack cooks, and old, soiled clothes were all that remained. The rest of the old, framed den was charred. It was a true reminder of the war zone this once was. His absence was a blessing to everyone here.

Phat had another house he'd used before that one burned. It was so much improved that I nearly passed it by. It was freshly painted, with green grass, blooming shrubs, and new fencing. As I spoke with the tenants, I learned they moved in only a few months ago and had no clue what used to go on there. I felt pretty good about things at that point, so I kept moving.

Tre had three houses he'd used down there. The first house I passed was also burned to the ground. There wasn't even enough left to board up. Across the street was the second house. That house had once been shot up in a drive-by just after Tre had moved out. It was all fixed up, with a new fence, paint, bullet holes repaired, and a new family inside. It was on the corner of Belzise and Talton Street, where I'd started making my first undercover buys. I remembered Tre coming out of the house with Candy that day and how excited and hopeful I felt about how this operation could turn out. I had no idea.

Across the street from Tre's second house was the house that watched over the south corner deals. It was situated next to the vacant wooded lot where a lot of the dope was hidden and where many of the street dealers found shade during the scorching summer heat. That house, too, was barely recognizable. It had a new everything but a roof. That red roof stuck out as always, but a new family was there taking good care of it. I decided to trek up the street to Tre's third, most infamous house, which championed the craziest stories.

I slowly pulled forward until I'd reached the intersection. What I saw at that moment made me nearly hit the curb in an overwhelming feeling of glorious amazement. A basketball goal with five little kids playing was in the cul-de-sac next to Tre's third house. I mean little kids, too. The youngest had to be maybe four, and the oldest, eight. What I felt in that moment I can't put into words. It was like I'd been painting a masterpiece on the side of a building for two years, part by part, until finally, the whole wall was filled. Then, I took the opportunity to step back, marvel at the big picture, and see how well all the parts had fit together, completing the masterpiece. And believe me, this sight made me feel like I'd painted a masterpiece. I literally parked my P.O.S. ride right there in the middle of the street and watched them play. They weren't worried about drive-by shootings or gangs. They didn't have a care in the world, which all kids deserve. I felt like I was in a completely different world. I was grateful for the opportunity to learn and contribute so much to this once-devastated area. There is always more to do, and I have learned so much from this that I feel more prepared than ever to keep advancing. The whole time I was under, I was equipping myself to carry a torch for the innocent, the persecuted, the discriminated. I didn't realize it then, but it was becoming clearer this day. My conviction to continue now seemed intrinsic.

Finally, I glanced over at Tre's spot; the same place I brought Carlos, the same place I'd met Tre to flip birds, the same place where so many guns had been used; it was amazing there weren't bodies buried here; the same place I met G-Pacc, my buddy and protector in the street; the same place D was shot when Stick kept robbing it. This very place now looked like frigging Martha Stewart had taken it over! It had new paint, new siding, a new picket fence to replace the chain link, new grass, new shrubs, and a new family to boot. I'll never forget.

After a few minutes, I decided to try to talk to a few more people. Amazingly, nearly everyone I spoke to that day was new to the neighborhood. They had either heard what happened but had no problems or didn't even know what I was talking about.

With the exception of the few stray LP family members on their corner, this place had transformed from a dilapidated, crime-ridden labyrinth of blood and coke to one with relatively carefree family activity, reasonably kept properties, and virtually no violent crime. I returned to repeat the same steps for the next two days, to make sure I wasn't seeing things. People who once lived there in fear were now freed of it. The new non-gang residents filled the empty spaces left by the scumbags who now lived in prison bunks. Even as recently as 2019, an FWPD supervisor informed me that the entire area in and around the Bowl is not even remotely as violent as it used to be.

By this time, Operation Fishbowl had been nominated for the FBI's case of the year. I was presented with the FWPD Officer of the Year award, the United States Attorney's Office Law Enforcement Commendation award, and I'd thrown out the first pitch at a Texas Rangers baseball game. My role was exposed as a few generous officers took it upon themselves to nominate me for these awards and bring what I contributed to light. Yet nothing meant more to me than this final realization that people's lives were truly changed for the better.

Although the impact was positive, hidden burdens were placed on some of the arrestees' families left behind. Families that once counted on dope money for financial support were now left high and dry. And although I didn't know good father figures in this operation, over 100 children were now left to grow up without one. They may be better off without the un-fatherly examples of their now-incarcerated sperm donors, but it will take a community effort. It will be a struggle for some of these boys and girls to find that important male role model that will provide positive reinforcement and accountability so they can overcome their unfortunate disposition and win. I think about those kids every day. Spouses, mothers, sisters, and brothers alike felt the unavoidable pain of the consequences set into motion by these gangsters. I hope they will learn as much from this as I have.

To ensure these children will be given the courage to step out of the cycle that brought their fathers to gang life, I know there is more for me to do. So, I am starting by donating all the profits from this book to organizations that mentor children of incarcerated parents.

I'll never forget the people, the invaluable lessons, the fortuitous relationships, and the most daring and soul-changing experiences of my life... in the Fishbowl.

Chapter 20
"WHERE ARE THEY NOW?"

This document, from 2006, is X-Man's Crip creed and marching orders to educate and focus his followers. We seized it from his home computer upon arresting him in our Fishbowl round-up.

5 x 2 Hoova Crips
This is the "G" code for all Crips. All Hoova Crips lay your eyes on this paperwork that's being set up for all Hoova Crips - not just Hoova Crips from Aggland, Hoovaland, Polywood, or Hoovawood

INTRODUCTION:
Welcome to the world of CRIP
This paperwork is to be consoled by the eyes of certified Hoova Crip Gang members only, violate any code & guidelines and that homie will be dealt with accordingly! Ft. Worth, Tx. Crips are like no other and our homies is luxury bound. Bustas & the enemy "cannot afford" to pay for, and therefore shall never enter a situation that'll cause the free lives of homies that are unaware of personal beefs to be taken. They know if they do, it will escalate this city to live to it's named L.A gang & crime unit: MurdA-Worth! Hoova Crip is definitely a notorious gang in our city and well respected by many.

Today, the way life is as a Hoova in Ft. Worth is a dangerous field to the uncertain but in the eyes of our world we're unfadeable with unity amongst our set (Hoova). Hoova has played many parts of our gang world in Ft. Worth! Hoova Crip's throughout the city have reclaimed sections & turf; which means: No Tresspassing by no means, whether enemy or potential enemy. Turfs such as: Polywood, Hoovawood, Hoovaland, & Aggland are the sections that are heard thru-out the state & institutions for deadly conduct, which means there are rida's with a mean & demanding respect for the turf. Your community will be safe by all means, that's why were sectioned off. Although there has been drama in the past with our own gang (Hoova), we strive to live for what's ahead.

Any homie that has been acknowledged, as a Hoova should be embraced, cause we live, ride, die and have cried for our Hoova Crip Gang! We have O.G.'s that over "C" the hood to make sho' thangs are done in a positive way in our eyes, but at the same time the law enforcement will criticize. Respect goes a long way homie. You can have civil life and citizens of all ages & race will support your actions in the hood. Everything we do isn't negative, we're stopping crime from outsiders, doing what's necessary for homies that's taken a fall for the hood, & making sho that upcoming homies don't live the life we lead, but embrace their thoughts.

As you all know May 2nd is our C-day homie! It's not a Crip party or picnic it's a family reunion to forgive & forget, but at the same time represent for the hood & the homies that'll no longer be with us during the season that's approaching (summer). Thang's get real hectic on the gang blast, and we all have to be cautious and well alert. Gang activity in Ft. Worth alone is bacc on the rise 56% as of March"06". We can't afford for another homie to be a statistic due to the negligence of a busta (enemy)! This call is by the O.G.'s that's upholding certain duties so "C" ya at family turf role call.

- *X-Man*

The 41 federal Fishbowl sentences total 629 years, 7 months, and one life sentence. Information gathered for the federal prosecution during the past 19 months resulted in nine cold-case homicides being investigated and some being prosecuted in state court.
--Bryon Okada, Fort Worth Star-Telegram, December 6, 2007

X-MAN
20 years federal prison without parole. He mourned the brutal execution of his wife and faced four murder charges with the state of Texas. He had it all. His millions are still out there somewhere, too.

TRE
20 years federal prison without parole. Tre was the first to be sentenced and continued to try to work his time down. He struggled with his slim chances after being one of the people that Phat forced into signing recantations of his original statements, thereby destroying any chances of becoming a good witness for the government. In November of 2007, he was stabbed four times despite being segregated in a maximum-security prison. Fortunately, he survived. Many of the cooperators face the same threats daily. Tre was finally moved to another state for his own protection. I hope gets his life together when he gets out.

NASTY
20 years federal prison without parole. He will serve this sentence after he completes his state time for aggravated assault of a family member. The DEA found thirty "kilo wrappings" with his fingerprints all over them. He was second in command to X-Man, the kingpin of the Operation Fishbowl conspiracy. At their peak, they were moving $250,000 worth of coke weekly.

PHAT
15 years federal prison without parole. After destroying many others' chances to help themselves by strong-arming them into signing in-jail documents, he finally cooperated by snitching out a couple of murderers and telling on his own crew. He received a 12-year break for his help. Hopefully, investigators will now look into him for raping his then 14-year-old girlfriend and stepdaughter of his ex-worker, JJ.

G-PACC
40 years federal prison without parole, following the remainder of a 27-year state sentence for Aggravated Robbery. Pacc received the biggest hit for signing Phat's documents in jail since he had not yet been sentenced before the signing and was facing the most time. Pacc's a bright, cool dude who may die in prison because he just couldn't quit. Ironically, I have continued investigating reasonable ways to get him freed before that happens. Intuitively, I believe he has much to contribute to society. If he can realize his potential as a man while inside, he will undoubtedly make a positive impact on our world.

GG
60 years federal prison without parole. He should not have gone to trial. GG proved to be a bigger thorn in my side than I'd ever expected, but the results speak for themselves.

YOLO
10 years federal prison without parole. He actually might have some potential as a productive member of society. Just a hunch, though.

TERENCE
20 years federal prison without parole. Terence had three kids within a year and a half with two different girlfriends. He contributed to my perspective about changing the mentality in some gang member circles that having a litter of children without any means or intention of support, is "cool."

JJ
19 years, 7 months federal prison without parole. His stepdaughter will now be safe from Phat. JJ passed on a break in his sentence by refusing to cooperate.

KADA
11 years federal prison without parole. How 'bout them Cowboys?

DANK

20 years federal prison without parole. Dank needed better advice. He refused to cooperate and tried to make up lies about other people he thought were lying about him. His credibility was damaged even further when members of his family and even his pastor got on the stand and blatantly lied for him. Since he worked under Tre, and Tre received a 20-year sentence, he also received 20, or he'd have gotten more. I'd hoped he would cooperate and get out sooner. I like Dank.

REGGIE

3 years federal prison without parole. Reggie got lucky. We missed a case that was still pending during his trial that would have allowed the judge to see him as the seller of dope he was instead of a poor user, which is precisely what his defense attorney claimed he was.

CUDA

10 years federal prison without parole. I like Cuda and have high hopes for his success when he gets out. He was the only person with a real job when we rounded everyone up. I also hope he manages to link Big Mask (the dirty cop) to something and bring the fool down. I never could pin him. Thankfully, he is now retired.

SICC

30 years federal prison without parole. He fought us and lost. He was also the one partially responsible for selling me the fake dope through Nado. The spelling of his street name is that way because in the gang world, putting "ck" together, as in the word siCK, represents "Crip Killer" on the street. He got 30 years. Good enough.

KENDRICK

10 years federal prison without parole. I really thought Kendrick would come through when this all went down, but he insisted we were targeting him simply because he was black. When he finally did admit he sold dope at all, he said he'd only sold to me and no one else, ever. He also said he decided to sell to me because it was too hard for a convict to get a real job. It is, indeed, harder for a convict to find a good job, and that is unfortunate. However, it cannot be leveraged as an excuse – only a reason. Hopefully, we, as a society, can change that equation so more of these guys can contribute when they get out instead of feeding the offender reciprocity epidemic. The whole "coach" defense certainly backfired, too, with Kendrick. I guess I was wrong about him.

ZULE
1 year, 5 months federal prison without parole. "Wow!" was all I could think as the Honorable (and very fair, I must add) Judge Means gave Zule a "time served" sentence, the most incredibly lenient sentence of them all. He based it on Zule's substantial cooperation, his perceived rehabilitation, including plans to counsel young inmates and the fact that word was out that he wouldn't survive 24 hours in federal prison because of a hit out on him for helping the government. The only thing not made apparent in the sentencing was the fact that he still awaited a state trial for the double shooting he did in 2005, which would have been a major consideration in the judge's decision had we been allowed to tell him that in court. The opportunity granted Zule comes only once in a lifetime. We can only hope he will cash in on it.

DEUCE
20 years federal prison without parole. Deuce worked on getting his time reduced but couldn't. He's in a maximum-security facility for violent offenders with Tre. In late 2010, he was stabbed multiple times, survived, and later transferred to another state. I'm glad this one went away - through-and-through, violent gangster.

D
7 years, 10 months federal prison without parole. D is quite the character. He's found Jesus and leads Bible studies in prison. He'd make a great preacher someday with his talents for telling a story. He utilized this ability in his sentencing as well, impressing the judge so much that he received a 10-year break for what most others were receiving three. Maybe there's some hope.

RAZOR
15 years federal prison without parole. His "click-clack" comment got him the "clink-clank" of locking prison doors for 15 long ones. Later, Razor.

Candy
2 years federal prison without parole. Candy was released in 2010. I still keep in touch with her family, who continue care for her children. I do truly hope that Candy will do well, but she'll need much support.

LIL' SAINT
20 years federal prison without parole. Lil' Saint had been skating dope cases all his life and was finally going to pay up. I guess he couldn't see his previous good fortune as a sign that maybe he should retire from the game. At his sentencing, he just stood there and said nothing. Worse, he kept mad doggin' the judge, who held Saint's future in his hands. I think he's been watching too many movies. The judge hammered him accordingly.

BIG STICK
30 years federal prison without parole and was also tried on two murders; one for killing the transvestite prostitute by the Fishbowl who neglected to tell him of his transformation until it was too late, and one for the murder of little Cedric's daddy. This one needs to stay gone.

BEELO
15 years, 8 months federal prison without parole. Beelo was a mild-mannered, easy-to-like gangster who tried to convince the judge he was harmless. He'd been poisoning Poly for years, and I'd been just missing him at his many dope houses prior to Operation Fishbowl.

LP
5 years, 10 months federal prison without parole. When he's released, his family still has a place for him in the Bowl, but I pray he won't go there. His legs were spared, and maybe even his life when he was rounded up because he had so greatly neglected his health (he used a neglected colostomy bag and a wheelchair). He was badly infected, and it took doctors a while to get him healthy again for trial. Despite him being a little older than most of these other cats, there is still plenty of time for good things to happen in his life…Fingers crossed.

BIG KILLA
LIFE + 5 years federal prison without parole. Not just the successor to his brother, Nasty's business after he'd been locked up, Big Killa faced a murder charge from the State of Texas for killing a 14-year-old boy with a bullet intended for a rival Blood gang member. He took us to trial on the Fishbowl charges and took the stand. It was his total undoing. He is a moron with a propensity for violence and is now gone for good. Following his loss in trial, he became so irate and belligerent that even his own attorney refused to meet with him unless Plexiglas was separating them. His sentence makes the world a safer place.

CED

15 years, 8 months. Hey, I never did get my TCU cap back! Ced was one of my favorite people in the whole operation. I honestly had no doubt he'd come clean and help himself in the end, but he refused the whole way through and got hammered for it. I really like the dude, and I hope he will get out and become a successful man.

And there's more. The rest of the Fab 41 didn't make the book but got their due all the same. Here they are:

BOOBIE

13 years federal prison without parole. Boobie is truly a hilarious dude. He had a rough upbringing in the Bowl. His mom sold crack down there for years. He wants more time off his sentence but has already received a break. Boobie is the kind of guy who could write his own book if he could ever succeed in the real world. But he'll need a full-time mentor and counseling to make it.

RED

20 years federal prison without parole. Red was a thorn in the side of Officer Caruthers and his beat. Caruthers did a great job tracking him down, and now he will be retired twice over when the Dog is loosed.

TRACE

19 years, 7 months federal prison without parole. Trace worked with Beelo and Kendrick, as well as several other big players in Poly.

TRELOW

20 years federal prison without parole. Trelow talked a big game on the street but was very personable in court, the opposite of most of these guys. I hate to see guys I like go down, but it's often necessary.

SWILLA

20 years federal prison without parole. Swilla was a Crip and dope-slinging underling of Deuce's in Poly, but no more.

SOMA

12 years federal prison without parole. Soma was Phat's right-hand man…back in the day.

CUZZO
2 years federal prison without parole. Cuzz ran Deuce's apartment near the Bowl where X-Man played ball on 4x3 Day. That got him hemmed up in this mess.

MENZA
5 years, 6 months federal prison without parole. Menza found Jesus, too, but his forte is singing. He sings at Bible studies and loves the opportunity to minister despite the fact that he thought he deserved a lighter sentence, which he didn't.

R.C.
12 years, 6 months federal prison without parole. Worked the old school block in the Bowl with Dominic, LouToc, and JJ. He's getting too old for this, so maybe he'll quit…Naaa.

LOUTOC
6 years federal prison without parole. He has a wife and a couple of cute kids waiting for him to come home. They'll need to move far away together when he's released to keep him focused on real-life success, not the game.

LIL' ONE
15 years, 6 months federal prison without parole. Lil' One was Sicc's cousin, and his best shot for a reduced sentence was to testify against him. He chose not to.

LOCO-MO
20 years federal prison without parole. Loco was just that, loco. He'd acquired a colostomy bag since I'd hung out with him last down on the Bowl blocks after losing a gun battle with some rival gangsters south of town. He'd walk around shirtless to show it off like it was a badge of honor or something. He was fun to hang with in the street, but he was belligerent and defiant as a defendant, and it cost him. He even tried to stare down Assistant United States Attorney Worley in court once. Got him 20.

BIG-C
8 years, 4 months federal prison without parole. We seized heroin, cocaine, and a couple of guns when we arrested him in the roundup. That didn't help him a whole lot. He also kept screaming, "I rebuke you in the name of Jesus!" at us as he was led out of the courtroom. I don't think he knew what he was saying, but if he did, I sure wasn't sweating it.

LORENZO
4 years federal prison without parole. He lived in Poly and had introduced me to some other bad guys I put on the hook. I don't think he likes me too much, but hopefully, he will learn from this experience.

DOMINIC
11 years, 8 months federal prison without parole. Dominic was a follower who worked the north blocks of the Bowl. At least he gets out before Phat, so he can consider going legit.

Last but not least, these important folks also had notable lives following this experience:

Bug
Bug returned to prison for a short stint after being caught up in a burglary. After that, he improved his life and moved away from the hood. I considered him a true friend. He worked a challenging job regularly and cared for his wife, dog, and one of his older children. But in the fall of 2015, he and his son were tragically killed in a boating accident. It was a gut shot. So many of his productive years are yet to give – taken away instantly. RIP, bro.

The Count
Yes, The Count; the rookie narc that wrecked the car into a pole during a staged pursuit. He got in trouble while driving around with weed in his undercover car and was banished to the Traffic Division for a couple of years, where he was assigned to work DWIs. A boneheaded supervisor still allowed him to return to narcotics despite his screw-ups and his tendency to drink as if he were a 16-year-old at a junior college party. One night, following a binge at a local bar, he drove and killed a mother of two. He served 20 years in state prison. Nice guy, but so sad.

Garrett Hull

Garrett was a Fort Worth police officer and an invaluable asset while I was dealing with Kendrick. He'd cover me while I rolled, gather intel, secretly track him down for me, and eventually be the guy that arrested him for me. I'd taught him much of what I knew as he took over some of the Weed and Seed ops after I went to Narc. He was good at what he did, and I trusted him with my life. After Fishbowl, we became very close friends, sparring partners, dinner pals with his wife and fam, and weightlifting compadres. Even more years later, he left the police department to join my security and investigations firm as one of my top managers. Ultimately, he would leave the firm and return to his true love - police work. But in the fall of 2018, while in a foot pursuit of three asshole bangers that had just robbed some poor souls at gunpoint, Garrett was shot and killed. He was a great officer and greater friend. Life is short and took a good one from us. RIP, my bro.

Me

I started another undercover project with full intentions of blowing it up even bigger than Fishbowl. I worked for several months as a crook amongst the "Mexican Mafia," originally an exclusive prison gang that spilled into the streets from California to Texas. I investigated and worked with a contact off the Gulf of Mexico who was an import/export source, moving bricks of coke into the U.S. with his other legitimate product. The project piqued the interest of upper management at the PD and FBI. With all the meddling, I was never granted the full amount of freedom and anonymity needed to make this succeed as Operation Fishbowl did.

So, I retired from the department in 2008 and founded Tactical Systems Network, LLC, an executive private security, investigation, and protection firm. It has been an entrepreneurial endeavor I do not regret, as it has presented new challenges for me. The firm is successful, and I am blessed to have been given these rare life opportunities.

Additionally, I produce music, video, and podcast projects. I often collaborate with other musicians and producers in artistic and entrepreneurial endeavors. To help bring systemic racism and injustices to light and further contribute to mentoring children of incarcerated parents. This is my new passion as I now walk with a unique disposition as a white nerd with a unique look into a culture that others like me do not have the advantage of experiencing.

Holli and I have never been closer. The tough times we survived as a team made us much stronger. I owe her my life for the remarkable love, patience, and support she brought then and continues to bring me with each new day. I am one lucky dude.

Regardless of any new endeavor I pursue, I shall remain forever changed by the remarkable people and harrowing experiences of my life in the Fishbowl.

AFTERWORD:
"WHAT CAN WE DO?"

I couldn't save X-Man's generation. I just ended up locking them away. But we must try to save those still in the streets. Another Operation Fishbowl should not be so necessary.

So, what can we do?

IN MY HUMBLE OPINION, there needs to be specific education in place for children of incarcerated parents. They need to be encouraged and mentored to overcome the odds they are working against, learn to be accountable to themselves and their peers, learn how to persevere against economic odds, be inspired to use their minds to combat our flawed, bigoted society intelligently; learn to love and respect themselves and others properly; become better than their parents. With mentoring and teaching at this level, they could listen to peers near their age, from the same hood, with broken homes and parents in jail, who know gangs and territories and, despite that, have created successful paths for themselves.

Very importantly, though, WE must then work to provide resources and opportunities for these under-advantaged kids. Simply telling them to "keep trying harder to beat the odds" amidst a broken, bigoted system without an effort from all sides is ignorant.

I truly do care that this cycle stops as it feeds into the cycles of violence I invested so much into halting and to which so many others have fallen victim. I think about the kids affected by Operation Fishbowl and the others just like them. My hope is that they will be fortunate enough to be touched by one of the people or organizations that support this cause. If we will all wake up and realize this issue affects so many more of us than we know, we can begin to move and make a change for children and our communities vital to our troubled nation's foundation.

To begin change, take action. I encourage you to support organizations that combat these issues or seek the opportunity to volunteer. Seek out and speak with other open-minded people – but not necessarily like-minded – and create productive discussions that prompt action and change. There is too much extremism going 'round these days. It is futile to spend time arguing with someone who has no interest in listening. There are plenty of us out here who want to engage and learn. Let's talk.

My website lists my favorite organizations that support children of incarcerated parents. To do my part, I am donating all of the profits from this book to those noble and caring entities.

SPECIAL THANKS:

The significant personal and professional contributions from the following people have proved invaluable:
Holli Broadwater, David Wilson, Bug (RIP, brother), Smurf, Pino, Jennifer Coffinadaffer, Mike Worley, Kelley Carruthers, Mark Ochsendorf, Scott Sikes, Rick Elston, John-John Ornelas, Marci, Darryl Cleveland, Stephanie Phillips, Barry Ragsdale, Chris Wolfe, Ralph Mendoza, Jerry Dalton, Kyle Jarrell, Tom Hughes, Frank Serra, Steve Hall, Garrett Hull (RIP, brother), Sutton McKee (post op), the FWPD Narcotics Unit, FWPD SWAT, the FWPD Gang Unit, Mark Thornhill, Lisa Ortiz, and Dale Ensley.
Also, a very special thanks to these journalistic and design geniuses for their dedicated time and mentoring during this book's writing, designing, and editing process: Jim Broadwater, Doug Swanson, Mark Moore, and Michael Precker.

AUTHOR BIO

Tegan Broadwater is a CEO, musician, entrepreneur, philanthropist, and author of "Life in the Fishbowl – The harrowing true story of one cop who took down 51 of the nation's most notorious Crips and his cultural awakening amidst a poor, gang-infested neighborhood."
Tegan's unique experience in the worlds of business, music, and rare deep
undercover work ignited a passion for contributing to positive change that has manifested in creative projects that purposefully spark productive conversations between different yet open-minded people.
Tegan spends most days running his businesses, recording thought-provoking tunes, investing time and money into his favorite charities, working out, writing, and sharing an occasional fine whiskey with his son or exclusive bros. But mostly, he enjoys spending invaluable time with his best friend and wife, Holli, just doing whatever [she wants].

Learn more about Tegan and his current doings at:
www.TeganBroadwater.com

Made in the USA
Columbia, SC
05 September 2024

41865724R00113